For David.

Bon Appetit.

Handle

May 2010.

Istanbul Contemporary Cuisine

Copyright:
© Hande Bozdoğan, Lâle Apa - 2009

Publisher

Apa Tasarım, Yayıncılık ve Baskı Hizmetleri AŞ
APA GIZ Plaza
Büyükdere Caddesi. No.191, 20th Floor
Levent 34330 İstanbul
Tel: +90 212 269 62 62 Fax: +90 212 283 23 10
uniprint@apa.com.tr

Concept Design
Genevieve Farez

Design & Layout
Yılmaz Aysan

Editor
Vildan Yahni

Food Photographer
Ahmet Ağaoğlu

Turkish/English Translation
Kenneth Dakan

Coordination
Peren Bilgin & Banu Özden

Printed by
APA-Uniprint Basım Sanayii ve Ticaret AŞ
Hadımköy- İstanbul Asfaltı, Ömerli Köyü
34555 Hadımköy, Çatalca Istanbul
Tel: +90 212 798 28 40

ISBN NO: 978-975-6845-17-2

2010
Gourmand
World Cookbook Awards
"Special Award
of the Jury"

Hande Bozdoğan - Lâle Apa

İstanbul
Contemporary Cuisine

Bizim
Mutfak

With taste and expertise.

Presented with the contributions of *Bizim Mutfak*.

Bon appetit.

Preface and Acknowledgements

At a time when the culinary sections of bookstores in Europe and North America are inundated with cookbooks featuring recipes from across the globe, there is surprisingly little on Turkish cuisine. The little that one may find is often subsumed in books on Mediterranean or Middle Eastern cooking.

The content of this cookbook emerged out of long discussions and exchanges of ideas regarding the unique characteristics of our cuisine. For us, it is a real treasure inherited over centuries from the rich culinary traditions of a vast geography once ruled over by the Ottoman Empire and further enriched today with cross-cultural influences from other world cuisines. The premise of the book is the fact that Istanbul is the indisputable home to the best of contemporary Turkish cuisine today, just as the best cooks of the Ottoman Empire worked in the palace kitchens of this magnificent city in the past. Hence, we wanted to offer a representative cross-section of the best and most popular dishes that Istanbulites with discerning palates enjoy on a daily basis, either at home or in one of their favorite restaurants which may range from a neighborhood eatery to one of the many internationally recognized higher-end establishments on Istanbul's vibrant culinary scene. We wanted such a cross-section to reflect Turkish cuisine's many cultural layers (including Armenian, Greek and Safarad dishes), diverse regional variations (from the distinct tastes of the Aegean to those of Southeastern Anatolia) and local idiosyncrasies (such as dishes from Konya or Kayseri kitchens), as well as the traces of its historical evolution (from classical Ottoman dishes to a contemporary fusion palette).

During the months that we worked on this book, Istanbul Culinary Institute offered us a home, library, laboratory, testing-kitchen, shooting studio and needless to say, plenty of inspiration. We invited the best chefs and leading food writers and critics of Istanbul to share some of their favorite recipes with us. They rolled up their sleeves for this project, selected a few dishes from their own menus or archives and personally prepared them in the Institute's demo kitchens where they were then photographed and their recipes recorded. To these we added a selection of our own recipes, choosing simple, familiar, healthy, and above all, tasty dishes that can be prepared easily with simple kitchen techniques and readily available seasonal ingredients. In the process, the pleasure of exchanging ideas with some of the best culinary talents in Istanbul and the pleasure of sampling these excellent dishes together turned into a memorable experience that we cherish as much as the pride of completing this book.

With two collaborating editors compiling 130 recipes from 30 leading chefs and food writers, this book could not have been produced without serious team-work and we owe thanks to many people who contributed to it in different capacities. We wish to express our heartfelt gratitude, first and foremost to the chefs and food writers who shared their recipes with us; to our dear friend Genevieve Farez who came up with the design concept and contributed indispensably to the French edition; to the master food photographer Ahmet Ağaoğlu with whom it is always a pleasure to work with; to the ever-talented Yılmaz Aysan who designed the book's layout; to Vildan Yahni, General Manager & Editor-in-Chief of The Guide Magazines and member of the Chaine des Rotisseurs, as her meticulousness was invaluable in editing the English version of the recipes; to the staff of Istanbul Culinary Institute who worked diligently to ensure that all the prep work was handled efficiently so that the chef's only had to prepare their dishes, especially to Banu Ozden who assisted us in every possible way; and to Peren Bilgin who graciously coordinated the work of this large team. We are grateful to the Istanbul Culture and Arts Foundation without whose support this project might not have been realized. Last but not least, we would like to thank our sponsor Bizim Mutfak, who has made it their mission to support the culinary arts and promote the joys of cooking to women from all walks of life.

We hope that our cookbook will give you a glimpse of the many exquisite tastes of an exciting city and will add new favorites to the recipe collections of cooking enthusiasts in Turkey as well as the rest of the world. No special skills or any hard-to-find ingredients are involved; anyone who loves good food and enjoys experimenting in the kitchen can prepare these recipes easily, wherever they are. Although we do believe that our book looks handsome on the coffee table, we hope that it will be heavily used in the kitchen: the more marked, underlined, highlighted and food stained the copies may end up, the more we will feel that we have accomplished our goal!

Hande Bozdoğan - Lâle Apa

Salads 22

Marinated Roasted Peppers
Gavurdağ Salad with Pistachios
Cacık(Yogurt &Cucumber)
Beet Salad
Citrus Salad
Aubergine Salad

Legumes 30

Chickpea and Sun-dried Tomato Casserole
Kuru Fasulye(White Bean Stew)
Akurdışışı (Bean Dip)
Chilled White Beans
Fava Soup
Chilled Wheat Berry Soup
Red Lentil Soup
Chickpea Soup with Spinach
Palace Chickpea Stew
Vegetarian Stuffed Grape Leaves
Topik (Layered Chickpea Pâté)

Vegetables 44

Spinach Root with Olive Oil
Asparagus and Artichoke with Jerusalem Artichoke Puree
Stuffed Vegetables with Olive Oil
İmam Bayıldı (Stuffed Aubergine)
Fried Aubergine with Tomato Sauce
Vegetable Medley with Olive Oil
Green Beans with Damson Plums and Olive Oil
Faux Stuffed Cabbage Stew
Artichoke Wrapped in Vine Leaves
Celeriac, Jerusalem Artichoke and Quince Rounds
Baba Ghanoush Terrine
Artichoke Soup with Olive Oil
Swiss Chard with Chickpeas
Carrots with Rice and Grape Molasses (Pekmez)
Cabbage with Walnuts
Zucchini and Aubergine au Gratin
Artichoke Salad
Stuffed Vine Leaves with Cherries

Pureed Peas with Samphire and Fresh Fava Beans
Baba Ghanoush with Goat Cheese Gratin
Grilled Halloumi in Vine Leaves
Stuffed Swiss Chard
Karnıyarık ("Slit Belly" Aubergines)
Stuffed Quince
Stuffed Artichokes with Chopped Meat
Marmarine
Artichoke with Olive Oil
Carrots with Cardamom and Olive Oil
Zucchini au Gratin

Savory Pastries 80

Onion Börek
Sigara Böreği(Cheese Cigars)
Gözleme (Swiss Chard Pastry)
Poğaça (Cheese Buns)
Açamuka (Cheese Pastry)
Pumpkin Fritters
Egg Noodles with Goat Cheese and Walnuts

Rices 90

Tomato Pilaf
Chicken and Almond Pilaf
Bulgur Pilaf with Chestnuts
Vegetable Bulgur Pilaf
Herbed Lamb Pilaf

Seafood 98

Pan-Fried Zander
Baked Crispy Sardines
Poached Sea Bass
Anchovy Croquettes
Stuffed Mussels with Saffron
Tiryaki Sauce
Sea Bass in Milk Sauce with Vegetable Mashed Potatoes
Stewed Octopus with Mastic
Swiss Chard Stuffed with Seafood
Octopus Carpaccio with Daikon and Celery
Baked Filet of Grouper with Vegetable Croquettes and Roasted Pepper Cream Sauce

Contents

Istanbul

Istanbul, the Enigmatic City and its Enticing Cuisine

Istanbul is rather like an onion. Layer by layer, it reveals a series of strata that stretch back into the mists of time. It is a huge city hosting millions of lives and thousands of different realities. Each region reveals a layer of Istanbul life - a slice of its cultural pie.

By Sevil Delin (with thanks to Tim Hindle)
Photos by Izzet Keribar, Ahmet Ağaoğlu, Ali Kabaş & Bahadır Tanrıöver

At its core lies its raison d'etre - the Bosphorus.

One of the most strategic straits in the world, it is also one of the most beautiful. Dividing Europe and Asia and connecting the Black Sea to the Marmara, it is spanned by two magnificent bridges. Ferries, yachts, tankers, cruise ships, speedboats, oil rigs, fishing boats, aircraft carriers, military ships and even the occasional rowboat vie for space on Istanbul's busiest artery. Istanbul's other famous stretch of water, the Golden Horn, is a freshwater estuary that divides the European bank and it gets its name from the color of its waters as the setting sun melts into it. An excellent natural harbor, it was home to the Byzantine and Ottoman navies.

Between the Bosphorus and the Golden Horn lies the triangular Sultanahmet peninsula, home to the Old City. This is where the best-known monuments, mosques and palaces are clustered. At its core stand the five pillars of historic Istanbul - Topkapı Palace, the Blue Mosque, the Haghia Sophia, the Hippodrome and the Basilica Cistern. Nearby, the legendary Covered Bazaar (also known as the Grand Bazaar) has over 4,000 tempting shops in its labyrinthine arcades. Sultanahmet is also home to the best-known museums, like the Museum of Turkish and Islamic Arts, the Archaeological Museum, Calligraphy Museum and Mosaic Museum.

In the past, Istanbul's European side consisted of the Old City plus a series of scattered districts and villages along its shores. These neighborhoods have merged into a seamless whole, but they still maintain a definite sense of individuality. As a result, the city has no center. No Place de la Concorde, no Times Square or Trafalgar Square. Instead, different activities are focused in different areas.

On the opposite shore of the Golden Horn to Sultanahmet, Istanbul peels off a layer to reveal a thoroughly modern face. The district of Beyoğlu is Istanbul's SoHo - a carnival of bars and restaurants, movie theatres and clubs, art galleries and bookstores, theatres and shops, churches, synagogues and mosques. The pedestrian Istiklal Caddesi (Avenue) forms Beyoğlu's backbone. Istanbul's most elegant, most obviously European neighborhood is nearby Nişantaşı, its streets packed with designer labels, stylish cafes, chic restaurants, trendy bars, elite boutiques and stunning Art Nouveau apartment buildings.

While much of its history and hubbub is centered on the European bank, many of Istanbul's residents live on its Asian shore. Here, you can witness the suburban lifestyle of Istanbul life, as well as a stunning view of the wonders on the opposite shore. Whether you drive over one of the two bridges or take a ferry across the Bosphorus, the journey to Asia is one you are guaranteed never to forget.

Just as Istanbul contains many different worlds, Turkish cuisine contains many different flavors. Istanbul is often called a melting pot of civilizations – a particularly apposite description when you consider its unique and delicious cuisine. Indeed, the Ottomans could be said to have invented the concept of fusion cooking. The Turkish kitchen is extremely varied, with every region, city and village having its own specialties. Local ingredients play a crucial role in dictating eating habits.

The Imperial Istanbul kitchen is the richest, incorporating all the finest flavors of the erstwhile Empire. The sultan's chefs were given the task of creating fare that would reflect the vast richness of its lands. The result was a unique cuisine that incorporated and redefined ingredients and preparations gathered everywhere from the steppes of Central Asia through to the Middle East, Mediterranean and Europe.

This "United Nations" of flavors is best appreciated in an array of appetizers called 'meze' that also include an international delegation of Greek, Armenian and Arab dishes. Meze are almost always served as an accompaniment to 'rakı', an aniseed-flavored drink that is Turkey's national tipple. The ultimate Istanbul triumvirate of flavors is meze, rakı and fish, best enjoyed at the city's fine shoreline fish restaurants.

Unlike in the West where soup is consumed primarily as a precursor to the afternoon or evening meal, in Turkey, soup can be consumed at any time of the day. Rather than being seen as an appetizer, it functions as a meal in itself. Soup is such an intrinsic part of Turkish psyche that it features in many proverbs and expressions: one may earn (in Turkish as well as English) one's "daily bread", but çorba parası or "soup money" is what Turks call the minimum amount needed to fill your stomach – and, tellingly, is slang for a bribe. The word çorbacı was the name of a superior rank among the Janissaries; when the Janissaries mutinied, as they often did, they would symbolically turn over the regimental soup cauldron, thereby refusing their ration and declaring their independence.

Turkey boasts excellent fresh vegetables, which are prepared in many ways, although Istanbulites prefer them as an accompaniment to a main meal and cooked in olive oil (another important ingredient in Istanbul cuisine) and served cold. Undoubtedly, Turks incorporated these olive oil vegetable dishes called 'zeytinyağlı' into their cuisine after their arrival in Asia Minor, as the vegetables and olive oil with which they are prepared are native to this region. Easy to prepare at home, delicious by themselves as a snack or as part of a traditional Istanbul repast, zeytinyağlı dishes are the pinnacle of refined Ottoman cuisine.

Thanks to its location on the shores on the Marmara and Black Seas, fish and crustaceans are a staple of the Istanbul diet. In Istanbul, fish is usually served whole, prepared grilled and served simply with a little lemon juice or steamed with vegetables as heavy sauces are considered to drown the natural flavor. A rocket (arugula) salad and some steamed potatoes make the simplest yet finest accompaniment.

Carnivores will be pleased to know that meat not only plays a dominant role in Turkish cuisine but is also equated with wealth, health, and even piety. The Kurban Bayram festival commemorating Abraham's willingness to sacrifice his son is marked by the slaughter of an animal, usually a sheep, whose flesh is then distributed to the poor and needy. In the past, Kurban Bayram may have been the only time of year that many Turks ate large amounts of meat. As meat in any variety was scarce and expensive, Turks developed the habit or using cheaper, smaller cuts such as mince or cubed meat. Larger cuts were usually only served at special occasions, such as wedding or circumcision festivities.

When referring to meat, or 'et' in Turkish, Turks usually mean lamb (*kuzu*) or mutton (*koyun*), the traditional mainstays, although veal (*dana*) and to a lesser extent beef (*sığır*) became popular in the second half of the

20th century. Nevertheless, most Turkish meat dishes are made, or are meant to be made, with lamb or mutton. Indeed, Turkey boasts some of the finest lambs in the world, the best of which comes from the Thrace region near Istanbul where they are fed on thyme, literally marinating their flesh as they grow.

At home, Turkish meat dishes are slow cooked with vegetables, resulting in a thick broth and delicious meat and vegetables that have imparted their flavors to each other. However, Turks also highly prize grilled meat, which is served well done, with no pink flesh or blood remaining in order to fulfill the traditions of Islamic halal dietary rules which prohibit the consumption of animal blood (animals are bled during slaughter). As this can result in dry, tasteless meat, Turks usually prepare grilled meats with vegetables and spices.

Without a doubt, the most famous Turkish dish is *kebap*. In Ottoman times the term kebap defined any meat, poultry, fish or seafood dish that was slow cooked in its own juice. But, over time, the wealth and variety of the Ottoman cuisine has eroded – much like its language – with many of the more colorful and evocative dishes such as oyster *kebap* disappearing. Today, there are hundreds of regional varieties of *kebap*. The most popular are made with lamb or chicken. The two best-known varieties of kebap are *döner* (turning) and *şiş* (skewer) kebap. As a rule, *kebap* dishes are spicier in the east and milder in the west of Turkey.

Cheese and yogurt play a major role in the Turkish kitchen. Originally, the Turkic tribes manufactured cheese and yogurt as a means of preserving and transporting milk during their long trek across Central Asia. The two most popular varieties are *beyaz peynir* (white cheese) - known internationally as 'feta' - and *kaşar peynir*, which is similar to mild

cheddar. *Beyaz peynir* makes up 70% of cheese production in Turkey. However, regional varieties made from cow, goat or sheep's milk abound and are worth seeking out.

Every kitchen in the world has its defining carbohydrates, and in Turkey they are phyllo pastry, bread and 'simit', a sort of bagel with a crunchy crust covered in sesame seeds. Phyllo pastry is used in both sweet and savory dishes, such as the ubiquitous 'baklava' and 'börek'. Bread is eaten at every meal, and might as well be considered a utensil as it is served with every bite. 'Simit' is the ultimate street food, a welcome snack either alone or with a piping hot glass of tea.

Turks are deservedly renowned for having a sweet tooth. It is for a good reason that Turkey is synonymous with the delectably divine 'lokum', introduced to the Western world as 'Turkish Delight' in the 19th century by a British traveler. The Ottoman palace kitchens also produced a wide range of mouth-watering, syrupy desserts. The best homemade baklava can consist of over 100 layers of translucent pastry. Baklava comes in a variety of shapes and fillings including walnuts, hazelnuts, pistachios, almonds, chestnuts, cheese, clotted cream and even chocolate. Turkey's favorite hard candy, *akide şekeri*, comes in a wide range of colors, shapes and flavors. *Akide* means 'a pledge of faith': in Ottoman times, the Janissaries presented *akide şekeri* as a symbol of their loyalty to the sultan. In fact, sugar is such an intrinsic part of the culture that a whole religious holiday is dedicated to sweets: the *Şeker Bayramı* or Sugar Holiday.

When it comes to beverages, wine has been an important part of life in Anatolia since as far back as 4000BC. The Hittites coined the term 'vino' around 1500BC. Back in Central Asia, the Turks were well acquainted with alcohol, their

spirit of choice being kımız, a drink made from mare's milk still drunk in the Turkic Republics. However, the production and consumption of wine fell into decline with their conversion to teetotal Islam in the 8th century and the gradual exodus of Greek and Armenian wine growers and enthusiasts. Turkey may be the fifth producer of grapes in the world, but only 4% of the harvest is turned into wine. Happily, the Turkish wine industry has been experiencing a long-awaited renaissance of late. Turkey boasts many native varieties of grape such as Öküzgözü, Boğazkere, Kalecik Karası and Narince.

Finally, Turks have been drinking tea and coffee for centuries. A thick, frothy Turkish brew goes to show that practice makes perfect. And perhaps the simplest way to experience local culture is to drink a glass of hot Turkish tea. Tea has remained a faithful friend to the Turks throughout their cross-continental history. As the Turkish social fabric frays, comes apart and is rewoven in a new pattern, you can always rely on tea to remain the same.

The child of Europe and Asia, Istanbul is a fascinating and flavorful blend of East and West. The explosion of new cafes, restaurants, bars and culinary establishments over the past ten years has turned the city into a gastronomic destination as visitors are drawn to discover its vast and varied cuisine. Fine chefs are continuing the Turkish trend started by the imperial kitchens of reinterpreting classic fare by incorporating new flavors and introducing new preparations. This book provides a wonderful opportunity to discover the essence of contemporary Istanbul cuisine, a combination of ancient flavors and modern imagination.

Salads

Marinated Roasted Peppers

Kıyı Restaurant

Preparation:

1. Roast peppers on an open flame or under the broiler, turning with tongs until all sides are charred. Place in a paper bag or wrap in foil; leave for about 15-20 minutes. Then carefully peel away the charred skin with your fingers or a paring knife. Remove stems and seeds.
2. Combine vinegar, olive oil, garlic and salt in a small mixing bowl.
3. Place the peppers in a shallow bowl and pour over the dressing. Cover and refrigerate.
4. Best marinated for two days.

Ingredients: (serves 6)

- 8 sweet red peppers
- 4 garlic cloves, crushed
- 2 tbsp red wine vinegar
- $^1/_3$ cup / 75 ml olive oil
- Salt, to taste

Gavurdağ Salad with Pistachios

Engin Akın

Preparation:

1. Wash tomatoes and dice into ¼ inch cubes.
2. Cut spring onions into ½ inch slices.
3. Remove the seeds from the banana peppers and slice into thin rings. Roughly chop parsley.
4. Combine the ingredients in steps 1-3 in a shallow bowl and add the pistachios and mix.
5. Add salt and pomegranate molasses just before serving and stir once again.
6. Garnish with roughly chopped mint leaves and serve.

Chef's note:

"Nar ekşisi" is a thick sweet-tart syrup sold in the USA and Europe as pomegranate molasses or syrup.

Ingredients: (serves 6)

- 4 firm tomatoes
- 4 spring onions (scallions)
- 2 sweet banana (yellow wax) peppers
- 1 small hot green pepper
- 4-5 sprigs flat leaf parsley
- ½ cup shelled green pistachios (or roughly chopped walnuts)
- 1 tbsp virgin olive oil
- 4 tbsp pomegranate molasses
- 12-15 mint leaves, chopped
- ¼ tsp salt

Cacık (Yogurt & Cucumber)

Lâle Apa

Preparation:

1. Peel and dice cucumbers.
2. Placed diced cucumbers in a colander, season with salt and let rest for 10 minutes.
3. Whip the yogurt in a separate bowl with a hand mixer.
4. Add garlic, white pepper, lemon juice and water (half a cup recommended) to the yogurt.
5. Then add diced cucumbers and stir.
6. Salt to taste and stir once more.
7. Spoon into six individual serving dishes. Drizzle a bit of olive oil over each serving. Garnish with dill and serve.

Chef's note:

Dill can be replaced with fresh mint or 1 teaspoon dried mint. The Greek word tzatziki is derived from the Turkish cacık, pronounced jah-juhk.

Ingredients: (serves 6)

- 4 medium cucumbers
- 1 tsp sea salt
- 3 ¾ cups / 750 g strained yoghurt
- 3 cloves garlic, crushed
- 1 tbsp lemon juice
- 2 tsp dill, finely chopped
- Olive oil
- White pepper, freshly ground

Beet Salad

Lâle Apa

Preparation:

1. Wash beets and remove stems and leaves. Place in a medium-size pot. Add enough water to cover the beets and bring to a boil on high heat. Then simmer for 15-20 minutes until tender.

3. Combine the sherry vinegar and salt in a large salad bowl. Rinse beets under cold water. Peel and cut into bite-size pieces while still warm. Combine with the sherry and salt mixture.

4. Combine the balsamic vinegar and lemon juice in a separate bowl. Stir continuously as you add the olive oil and freshly ground black pepper.

5. Just before serving, pour the dressing over the beets and stir.

6. Garnish with lemon peel and serve.

Chef's note:

Apples, pears, oranges and roasted hazelnuts or walnuts are good acccompaniments for beets.

Ingredients: (serves 6)

- 1 lb / ½ kg beets
- 1 tsp lemon juice
- 3 tbsp olive oil
- 1 tsp balsamic vinegar
- 1 tbsp sherry vinegar
- 1 tsp ground salt
- 1 tsp ground black pepper
- Lemon peel, for garnish

Citrus Salad

Deniz Alphan

Preparation:

1. Peel oranges with a paring knife. Slice into rounds and place in a salad bowl.
2. Combine olive oil, lemon, salt and spices to make dressing, adjusting quantities and ratios as desired.
3. Add thinly sliced red onion and capers to the dressing and wait 10 minutes for the flavors to marry.
4. Pour the dressing over the orange slices half an hour before serving.

Ingredients: (serves 6)

- 3 medium oranges
- 1 large red onion
- 3 tbsp olive oil
- 1 tbsp lemon juice
- 1 heaping tsp capers
- Dash of cumin
- Dash of black pepper
- ½ tsp hot paprika
- Dash of salt

Chef's note:

"Pul biber", a moderately hot paprika widely used in Turkey, is available at some specialty spice shops and Middle Eastern grocers abroad. It's similar to "Aleppo" pepper.

Aubergine Salad

Borsa Restaurant

Preparation:

1. Roast the globe aubergines (See page78); reserve the other aubergines for step 5.
2. Combine olive oil, salt, sugar and lemon juice in a bowl.
3. Peel the aubergines and add to the dressing in step 2. Mash with a wooden spoon for 3-4 minutes until pureed.
4. Grate the cheese for the crackers. Combine with cornmeal and sauté in a non-stick saucepan until brown on both sides. Cut into six long strips.
5. Cut the reserved aubergines into thin lengthwise strips. Grill on both sides on a barbeque or under the broiler. To serve, place a serving of the aubergine puree in the center of a dish. Take one strip of the grilled aubergine and place around the aubergine puree. Tie the serving with a piece of the green part of a spring onion to secure. Garnish with a cheese cracker and cherry tomato and serve warm.

Chef's note:

"Eski kaşar" is an aged, yellow, sharp cheese made from sheep's milk. Semi-hard melting cheeses such as provolone, kashkaval and kasseri can also be substituted.

Ingredients: (serves 6)

- 2 kg globe aubergines
- 2 aubergines
- 1 tbsp virgin olive oil
- 1 tbsp powdered sugar
- 2 tsp salt
- 1 lemon, juiced
- 6 fresh chives or spring onions (scallions) and cherry tomatoes, for garnish

For crackers:

- 1 cup grated aged kaşar cheese
- ½ tbsp cornmeal

Legumes

Chickpea and Sun-dried Tomato Casserole

Istanbul Culinary Institute - İsmail Özkapu

Preparation:

1. Soak dried chickpeas overnight or for at least 8 hours in water and drain. In a pot, boil in water for 20-25 minutes, until partially cooked.
2. Soak the sun-dried tomatoes in a bowl of hot water for half an hour.
3. Finely chop onions and in a saucepan, sauté in butter and sunflower oil. When they become translucent, add tomato paste and stir. Add the sun-dried tomatoes and continue to sauté for a few minutes.
4. Heat the oven to 180°C/350°F.
5. Drain the chickpeas and place in an earthenware casserole dish. Spoon the tomato and onion mixture over the chickpeas and pour in the vegetable (see page 79) or chicken stock. Season with salt and black pepper to taste.
6. Cover the casserole with aluminium foil and bake for 30 minutes.
7. Serve hot in the casserole garnished with a few sprigs of fresh thyme.

Ingredients: (serves 6)

- 2 ½ cups chickpeas
- 2 cups sun-dried tomatoes
- 2 tbsp tomato paste
- 2 medium onions, chopped
- 4 cups vegetable or chicken stock
- 2 ½ tbsp butter
- 1 ½ tbsp sunflower oil
- Salt, to taste
- Black Pepper, to taste
- Fresh thyme, a few sprigs for garnish

Kuru Fasulye (White Bean Stew)

Istanbul Culinary Institute

Preparation:

1. Soak white beans in water overnight and drain.
2. In a pot, boil in water for 30 minutes.
3. Heat butter in a pot, add onions and sauté. When the onions become translucent, add the peppers.
4. Add the sun-dried tomatoes and, after 1-2 minutes, the tomato paste.
5. Add the white beans, beef stock or water and season with salt. Simmer covered for 30 minutes.
6. Sprinkle with hot paprika and serve.

Ingredients: (serves 6)

- 3 cups white beans
- 100 g / 7 tbsp butter
- ½ cup sun-dried tomatoes, thinly sliced
- 2 onions, finely chopped
- 4 banana (yellow wax) peppers, diced
- 6 tbsp tomato paste
- 3 cups beef stock or water
- Hot paprika, to taste
- 1 ½ tbsp salt

Chef's note:

Kuru fasulye is usually served on a bed of plain white rice with a side of sour and salty pickles. You can also garnish the dish with oregano.

Akurdışışı (Bean Dip)

Zeynep Çelikkan Kakınç

Preparation:

1. Cook the fresh beans in boiling water for a few minutes. Drain and place in pot.
2. Add hot paprika, 1 coarsely chopped onion, coriander, garlic, wild thyme, salt and water to cover. Bring to a boil and reduce to medium heat. If necessary, add more water and cook until the beans are tender.
3. Finely chop the other onion and sauté in butter until translucent in a saucepan.
4. Place the beans in a food processor or blender and mix at the lowest speed.
5. Place in a serving dish.
6. Pour the butter and onion mixture over the beans.
7. Garnish with chopped spring onions and serve.

Chef's note:

A large tan bean streaked with black and red , called "barbunya" in Turkish - or fresh cranberry beans are also known as Barlotti beans or Roman beans and shouldn't be confused with pinto beans. Dried beans can be substituted for fresh.

Ingredients: (serves 6)

- ½ kg fresh cranberry beans, shelled
- 2 large onions
- 1 large clove garlic
- 4 ½ tsp hot paprika
- 4 ½ tsp coriander
- 4 ½ tsp dried thyme
- ¾ bunch spring onions (scallions)
- 2 tbsp butter
- Salt, to taste

Chilled White Beans

Kıyı Restaurant

Preparation:

1. Soak beans in water overnight and strain. In a pot, boil in water until cooked 'al dente' and strain.
2. In a separate pot, sauté the onions in sunflower oil until light brown. Add tomato paste, salt and hot paprika and continue stirring for 2-3 minutes and add water. Stir in the beans and simmer for one and a half hours on low heat.
3. Remove from heat. As the beans cool, stir periodically to keep the oil evenly distributed.
4. Chill in a serving dish for a day in the refrigerator and serve cold.

Chef's note:

If you prefer to serve hot, sauté the boiled beans in a heaping tablespoon of butter, ¾ tsp hot paprika and ¾ tsp thyme. Spoon the beans into a casserole and bake in a preheated oven at 180˚C/350˚F until tender.

Ingredients: (serves 6)

- 2 ½ cups large white beans (Dermason or Great Northern are best)
- 1 ¾ cups sunflower oil
- 5 tbsp tomato paste
- 2 medium onions, grated
- ½ tsp cayenne pepper
- ½ tsp salt
- 1 ²/₃ cups water

Fava Soup

Istanbul Culinary Institute

Preparation:

1. Wash the carrot, potato and onion and cut into large cubes.
2. Heat sunflower oil in a large pot and add, in turn, the onion, carrot, potato and fava beans. Sauté for a few minutes.
3. Add vegetable stock and bring nearly to a boil. Then lower the heat and simmer until the carrot and fava beans are tender.
4. When the vegetables are fork tender, blend them with the cooking liquid in a blender or force the vegetables through a strainer. Season with salt and black pepper. 5. If the soup is too thin continue cooking until it reaches the desired consistency. Garnish with the dill and serve.

To make the vegetable stock:

Cut the vegetables into chunks and add to a large pot of boiling water. Cook on medium heat until tender. Strain and reserve the cooking liquid.

Ingredients: (serves 6)

- 2 cups dried fava beans
- 1 medium potato
- 1 medium onion
- 1 medium carrot
- 2 tbsp sunflower oil
- 2 tbsp butter
- 2 lt. vegetable stock
- ¼ bunch dill, chopped
- Salt, to taste
- Black Pepper, to taste

For the vegetable stock:

- 2 lt water
- 1 celeriac
- 1 carrot
- 1 leek
- 1 onion
- 1 tomato
- 6-7 sprigs flat leaf parsley

Chilled Wheat Berry Soup

Istanbul Culinary Institute

Preparation:

1. Soak the wheat berries in water for six hours and drain. Then boil in water until tender and strain.
2. Boil the vegetable stock (See page 78) in the pot you're using for the soup, then reduce heat to low.
3. Whip the yogurt and egg in a bowl. Stir in a bit of the heated stock to warm the mixture. Then slowly add the yogurt to the stock, stirring continuously. Season with salt and black pepper.
4. Add the wheat berries. Simmer for a few more minutes and check the seasoning.
5. Heat olive oil in a small saucepan, add mint and turn off the heat immediately. Pour over the soup and stir once. When the soup has cooled, place in the refrigerator. Serve chilled.

Ingredients: (serves 6)

- ¾ cup soft wheat berries
- 1 lt vegetable stock
- 1 cup strained yogurt
- 1 egg
- 4 tbsp olive oil
- 1 tbsp dried mint
- Salt, to taste
- Black Pepper, to taste

Red Lentil Soup

Istanbul Culinary Institute

Preparation:

1. Rinse the lentils in plenty of water and drain.
2. Rinse and roughly chop the potato, onion and carrot. Heat olive or sunflower oil in a pot. Add and sauté the vegetables for a few minutes and then add the lentils.
3. After a few more minutes, add vegetable (see page 78) or beef stock, cumin, black peppercorns and season with salt.
4. Once the vegetables are tender, use a hand blender to mix until smooth.
5. In a separate small saucepan, sauté flour in butter until golden. Stir mixture into the soup.
6. Stir well, dilute the soup if it's too thick and serve hot.

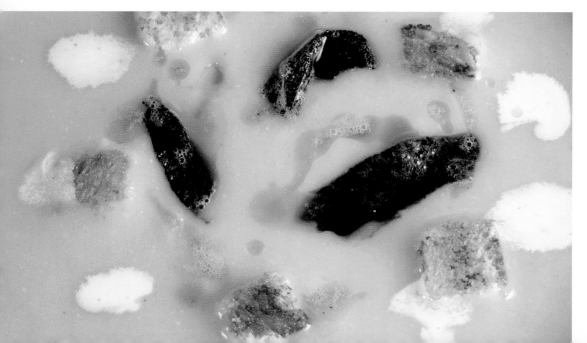

Ingredients: (serves 6)

- 1 cup red lentils
- 1 medium carrot
- 1 medium yellow onion
- 1 medium potato, peeled
- 1 tbsp salt
- 1 ½ tsp black peppercorns
- 1 tbsp cumin
- 50 ml olive or sunflower oil
- 2 ½ tbsp butter
- 1 ½ tbsp flour
- 2 lt beef or vegetable stock

Chickpea Soup with Spinach

İnci Birsel

Preparation:

1. Soak chickpeas for 12 hours, drain and rinse in fresh water. Place 9 cups of water, chickpeas, beef bone , 2 cloves garlic and half an onion in a large pot. Cook until the chickpeas are tender, adding more boiling water if necessary.
2. Drain and puree half of the chickpeas in a food processor or blender and place in a pot.
3. Add the remaining whole chickpeas (skins peeled if desired) and season with salt and black pepper.
4. Heat olive oil in a separate saucepan. Add the remaining onion (grated) and crushed garlic and sauté until translucent.
5. Add the rinsed, finely chopped spinach leaves to the saucepan and stir until spinach is bright green and tender.
6. Add the spinach mixture to the pot of chickpeas. Add the chicken stock and stir until the stock is piping hot. Add more salt and black pepper if desired.
7. Drizzle a little olive oil and sprinkle a teaspoon of grated Parmesan cheese to each individual serving.
8. If you enjoy spicy food, add some cayenne pepper or hot paprika.

Ingredients: (Serves 6-8)

- 2 cups chickpeas
- 9 cups water
- 2 large onions
- 2 cloves garlic
- 1 large beef bone
- 4 tbsp olive oil
- 3 cloves garlic, crushed

- ½ kg / 3 cups spinach leaves, rinsed and finely chopped
- 1 lt chicken stock
- ¼ cup Parmesan cheese, freshly grated
- Sea Salt, to taste
- Black Pepper, freshly ground, to taste

Palace Chickpea Stew

Engin Akın

Preparation:

1. Boil the pre-soaked chickpeas in plenty of water until tender.
2. Remove from heat, remove skins and blend chickpeas in a food processor, adding stock if needed.
3. Add the hot stock of your choice to chickpeas. The mixture shouldn't have an overly smooth consistency.
4. Ladle into individual bowls, sprinkle each with a pinch of cinnamon and drizzle with some melted butter or olive oil.

Preparation of the stock:

Cut the vegetables into large chunks and add to a large pot of boiling water. When they're tender reduce heat to medium and continue cooking until they're soft. Force the cook vegetables through a sieve, reserving the cooking liquid.

Note: This soup thickens as it rests, so we advise serving it on the thin side.

Chef's note:

This recipe is an interpretation of one found in nearly all cookbooks written in the 18th and 19th centuries. My inspiration was a memorable bowl of soup I savored one night at La Bottega del 30, a Tuscan restaurant in a small village in Sienna. I was able to find an Ottoman recipe for a similar dish. The only difference is that rosemary is replaced with cinnamon in the Ottoman recipe.

Ingredients: (serves 6)

- 2 cups chickpeas, soaked overnight
- 6 cups vegetable stock (beef or chicken can be substituted)
- Salt, to taste
- 2 tbsp olive oil or melted butter
- 2 tsp cinnamon, ground

For vegetable stock:

- 1 lt water
- 1 celeriac
- 1 carrot
- 1 leek
- 1 onion
- 1 tomato
- 6-7 sprigs flat leaf parsley
- 1 cinnamon stick, optional

Vegetarian Stuffed Grape Leaves

Takuhi Tovmasyan Zaman

Preparation:

1. Remove the grape leaves stems. If fresh, rinse. If from a jar, drain the brine and rinse well under cold running water. Then soak in hot water for an hour and drain.

2. Remove any foreign objects from lentils and rice, rinse and soak in water.

3. Dice the onions and sauté in a saucepan on low heat with a sprinkle of salt. Reserve for later.

4. Drain lentils and rice.

5. For the filling of the grape leaves, add a half cup of olive oil, the juice of half a lemon, hot paprika, dried mint, lentils, rice and sugar to the cooked onions. Stir well. If you wish, add more seasoning to taste.

6. To stuff the grape leaves, place a leaf, shiny side down, vein side up in the palm of your hand Place a tablespoon of the filling in the center stem end of the leaf. Form the leaf into a compact little bundle by folding in the tips of the top two leaves, one atop the other. Then, fold in the sides and roll the bottom up and over for a tight fit. Repeat with the remaining leaves until you've used up all the filling.

7. Line the bottom of a large pot with any torn or tough leaves and place the stuffed leaves in concentric circles, leaving as little space as possible, with as many layers as necessary.

8. Drizzle half a cup of olive oil and the juice of half a lemon over the grape leaves.

9. Place a flat, heatproof plate over the grape leaves, in the pot, to keep them from moving around as they cook.

10. Cover and cook on medium heat for a few minutes, then reduce to low and simmer for one and half hours.

11. When the grape leaves have cooled completely, arrange on a serving dish and serve.

Ingredients: (serves 6)

- 1 jar grape leaves or 250 g large fresh leaves
- 1 cup red lentils
- 2 tbsp rice
- 1 kg onions
- 2 tsp salt
- 1 cup olive oil
- 1 lemon, juice of
- 2 tsp hot paprika
- 2 ½ tsp dried mint
- 2 tsp sugar
- 2 cups water

Topik (Layered Chickpea Pâté)

Takuhi Tovmasyan Zaman

Preparation:

1. Soak the chickpeas overnight and drain.
2. In a pot, boil chickpeas in water until tender. Drain, remove the skins and mash.
3. Wash potatoes and in a pot of warter boil with skins until tender. Peel, add to chickpeas and mix until it reaches a paste-like consistency.
4. Add salt, sugar, cinnamon and tahini and knead with your hand until thoroughly mixed.
5. Finely chop the onions. In a saucepan, sauté on low heat (do not add oil), stirring occasionally, until caramelized and reduced by about two-thirds, in terms of volume.
6. Add onions to a bowl containing the currants and pine nuts. Add cinnamon, allspice, black pepper and sugar. Mix well and allow mixture to cool.
7. Lay out 6 pieces of plastic wrap, the size of a handkerchief. Divide the chickpeas and onion filling into 6 equal portions.
9. Place a small portion of mashed chickpea on a piece of plastic wrap and roll out to the thickness of an orange peel. Then spread a serving of the onion filling into each portion. With the help of the plastic wrap, make a small package of each portion.
10. Refrigerate in the plastic wrap for a day. Then remove from plastic wrap and score each portion into 4 equal pieces.
11. Drizzle a tablespoon of lemon juice and olive oil and sprinkle with a generous amount of cinnamon.

Ingredients: (serves 6)

- 1 cup chickpeas, dried
- 2 large potatoes
- 2 tsp salt
- 2 tsp sugar
- 2 tsp cinnamon
- ½ cup tahini

For the filling:

- 1 ½ kg onions
- 2 tsp salt
- 2 tbsp currants, soaked
- 2 tbsp pine nuts, rinsed
- 4 tsp cinnamon
- 2 tsp allspice
- 2 tsp black pepper
- 2 tsp sugar
- 1 ½ cups tahini
- plastic wrap

Chef's note:

Topik is a classic dish created by Anatolian Armenians. It can be enjoyed on its own or as a meze (appetizer).

Vegetables

Spinach Root with Olive Oil

Istanbul Culinary Institute

Preparation:

1. Rinse spinach roots.
2. Heat olive oil in a large pot.
3. In turn, sauté the onion, garlic and carrot. When the vegetables are tender, add spinach roots and continue to sauté.
4. Add the cubed tomato and sauté for a few minutes longer.
5. Add vegetable stock. Season with salt, black pepper and sugar.
6. Place a sheet of wax paper over the pot and cover the lid.
7. Simmer for 15 minutes, add the lemon, stir once and remove from heat.
8. Serve at room temperature or chilled.

Chef's note:

When making dishes with spinach leaves only, do not throw away the roots so that you can use them later in tasty, simple recipes like this one.

Ingredients: (serves 6)

- 1.25 kg spinach roots
- 240 g / 1 medium onion, finely chopped
- 1 clove garlic, finely grated
- 75 g / 1 medium carrot, grated
- 120 g / 1 medium tomato, diced
- 50 ml / ¼ cup olive oil
- 125 ml / ½ cup vegetable stock
- 1 lemon, juice of
- Salt, to taste
- 1 tsp black pepper
- 2 tsp sugar
- 1 sheet wax paper

Asparagus & Artichoke with Jerusalem Artichoke Puree

Gönül Paksoy

Preparation:

1. Clean artichokes. (See page 79). Peel onions.
2. Cook artichokes and the whole peeled onions in a pot with 50ml of the olive oil, water, sugar and salt.
3. When artichokes are tender, add the asparagus and cook for another 3-4 minutes.
4. Peel the Jerusalem artichokes and in a pot of water boil until soft. Then mix to form a chunky puree.
5. Finely chop dill.
6. Add remaining olive oil and dill to the puree and season with salt and white pepper.
7. Arrange the artichokes on a bed of Jerusalem artichoke puree. Garnish with onions and asparagus. Serve chilled.

Chef's note:

Tender green asparagus can be used instead of white.

Ingredients: (serves 6)

- 6 globe artichokes
- 4 medium yellow onions
- 100 ml / ½ cup olive oil
- 75 ml / ⅓ cup water
- 3 tbsp sugar
- 12 white asparagus
- 12 Jerusalem artichokes
- 1 bunch dill, chopped
- ½ tsp white pepper, ground
- Salt, to taste

Stuffed Vegetables with Olive Oil

Istanbul Culinary Institute

Preparation:

To prepare the tomatoes:
1. Cut off stems of the tomatoes to make a "lid".
2. Completely hollow out the tomatoes and put to one side, along with their lids

To prepare the peppers:
1. Cut off the dark green area at the stem of the bell pepper and remove the seeds.

To prepare the aubergines:
1. Cut 4-5 cm off the stem of the aubergines. Use the tip of a sharp knife to hollow out some of the flesh, being careful not to puncture the skin.
2. Place aubergines on the counter top and roll back and forth, pressing down lightly with your hand to loosen up the remaining flesh and seeds. Hollow out the remaining flesh.
3. Reserve a 2cm "plug" of flesh for each aubergine to use as a lid.

Vegetable filling:
1. Heat about a half a cup of water or vegetable stock in a pot (see page 79).
2. In a separate saucepan, roast pine nuts in hot olive oil until golden and add onions.
3. Once onions are fully caramelized, add rice and sauté for 6-7 minutes. Add, in turn, currants, salt, sugar and hot water or vegetable stock. Continue cooking on low heat until the liquid is absorbed.
4. Remove from the heat, add allspice, cinnamon, dill, mint and parsley, then fluff with a spoon and let sit.
5. Use equal amounts of the mixture to stuff the pre-prepared vegetables.

To cook the stuffed vegetables:
1. Arrange stuffed vegetables in a large pot. Add the remaining vegetable stock and olive oil. Cover the top of the vegetables with a sheet of wax paper small enough to fit inside the pot. Simmer covered on low heat until the vegetables are tender.
2. Place the vegetables on a serving dish and pour the pan drippings over them. Served chilled.

Ingredients: (serves 6)

- 1 cup rice, soaked
- 3 tbsp currants, soaked
- 3 tsp pine nuts
- 1 tbsp allspice
- 1 tbsp cinnamon, ground
- ¼ bunch dill, finely chopped
- ¼ bunch mint, finely chopped
- ¼ bunch parsley, finely chopped
- 2 large yellow onions, grated
- 1 tbsp sugar
- ¾ cup olive oil
- ¾ cup hot water or vegetable stock
- Salt, to taste
- Wax paper, to cover pot
- 2 medium tomatoes
- 2 medium green bell peppers
- 2 medium long thin (Japanese) aubergines

Chef's note:

The cooking times for the three vegetables differ, so we recommend cooking them separately. If you do cook them together, remove each vegetable from the pot as soon as it becomes tender. This dish is more flavorful after it has been chilled for a day or two.

Imam Bayıldı (Stuffed Aubergine)

Beyti Restaurant

Preparation:

1. To give a striped effect to the aubergines, peel off the skins lengthwise - about a finger lenght apart. Soak aubergines in salted lemon water for 30 minutes.
2. Cut onions in half and then into thin slices. In a saucepan, sauté onions, red bell pepper and garlic in sufficient olive oil until thoroughly cooked and add the tomatoes.
3. Stir in tomato paste, sugar and flour. Season with black pepper, curry powder and cumin and cook until the mixture reaches the consistency of a thin paste. Season with salt, add water and cook on high heat for 10-15 minutes.
4. Place in a fine strainer over a bowl. Mix in the chopped parsley and dill and allow the excess liquid to drip through the strainer.
5. Remove aubergines from the salted lemon water and rinse in fresh water. Squeeze off any excess liquid, pat dry. In a saucepan, heat olive oil and fry on both sides. Place in a baking tray and use the handle of a spoon to create a lengthwise slit in the flesh of each aubergine.
6. Spoon the tomato mixture into the slits and decorate each aubergine with a slice of tomato and banana (yellow wax) pepper.
7. Pour liquid that filtered through the strainer over aubergines. Bake on the bottom shelf of the oven until the tomato and pepper garnish has browned.

Chef's note:

If the aubergines are bitter, you can sprinkle a tablespoon of sugar over them after frying. Imam Bayıldı literally means "the imam fainted", although there is disagreement over whether the Muslim holy man fainted over the succulence of the dish or the cost of the olive oil used to prepare it.

Ingredients: (serves 6)

- 6 long, thin (Japanese) aubergines
- 2 yellow onions
- 1 green bell pepper
- 1 red bell pepper
- 1 banana (yellow wax) pepper
- 2 tomatoes, finely diced
- 2 cloves garlic, grated
- ¼ tsp black pepper
- ¼ tsp curry powder
- ¼ tsp cumin
- 1 tbsp tomato paste
- 1 tbsp sugar
- 2 tsp flour
- 2 cups water
- Olive oil for frying
- 1 bunch flat leaf parsley
- 1 bunch dill
- Salt, to taste

Fried Aubergines with Tomato Sauce

Lâle Apa

Preparation:

1. Peel the aubergines in lengthwise strips a finger wide to give a striped effect. Sprinkle with salt, cut diagonally into ovals. Let stand for 20 minutes, then rinse and drain. Pat dry with paper towel.
2. Remove stems and seeds from green bell peppers and quarter.
3. In a saucepan, heat sunflower oil and fry aubergines and green bell peppers until they turn golden brown. Remove with tongs and place on paper towel.
5. Peel and remove the seeds of the tomatoes. Boil the tomatoes in a saucepan until they reach a soft and smooth consistency.
6. Add sugar, crushed garlic cloves and balsamic or white wine vinegar.
7. Season with sea salt and black pepper to taste.
8. Spread tomato sauce on a serving dish. Layer aubergines and peppers on the sauce, one atop the other, like a tower.
9. Garnish with basil leaves.
10. If desired, serve strained fat-free yogurt on the side or sprinkle grated fresh parmesan cheese.

Ingredients: (serves 6)

- 600 g / 6 aubergines
- 4 green bell peppers
- Sunflower oil, for frying
- 6-7 ripe medium tomatoes
- 5 cloves garlic, crushed
- 2 cubes sugar
- 1 ½ tbsp balsamic or white wine vinegar
- 5-6 leaves basil
- Sea salt, to taste
- Black Pepper, freshly ground, to taste

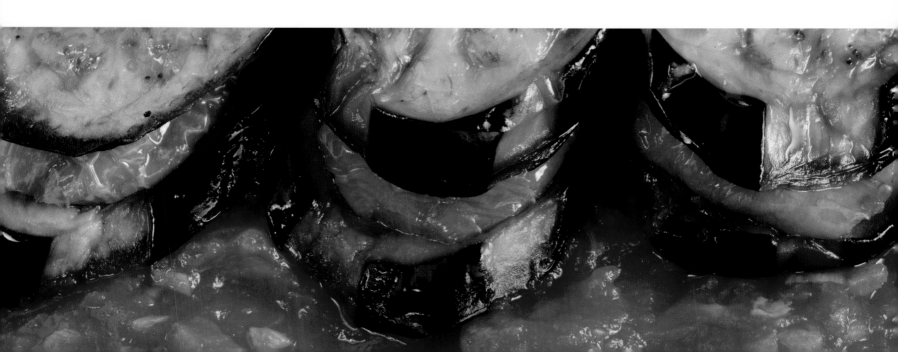

Vegetable Medley with Olive Oil

Hülya Ekşigil

Preparation:

1. Peel alternating finger-width strips of the aubergines. Cut into lengthwise slices and place in a bowl of water, seasoned with 1 teaspoon salt.
2. Peel the skins of the tomatoes, remove seeds and dice.
3. Place 2 tablespoons olive oil and ¼ cup hot water in a stainless steel pot.
4. Put the whole peeled onion in the middle of the pot and arrange the green beans around it.
5. Spoon ¾ of the diced tomatoes into the spaces around the edges of the pot. Sprinkle 1½ teaspoon of salt over the vegetables. Place a heat proof plate inside the pot on top of the vegetables. Cover with the lid and cook for 10 minutes on medium heat and 20 minutes on low heat.
6. Meanwhile, remove the aubergines from the water, squeeze off any excess water and pat dry. Fry the aubergine slices on one side only in ½ cup of olive oil.
7. Peel alternating strips of the zucchini and slice lengthwise.
8. Cut the red bell pepper into eight pieces.
9. After the beans have cooked for an hour, remove the plate. In the same pot, add a layer of zucchini and red bell pepper.
10. Add a layer of aubergine, with the fried side facing upwards.
11. Sprinkle ½ teaspoon salt and 2 teaspoons sugar over the vegetables. Mix the remaining diced tomatoes and basil and pour over the vegetables. Cook on medium heat for 25-30 minutes.
12. When the pot has cooled sufficiently, removed the lid and use a plate to keep the vegetables in place as you pour out the liquid into a small frying pan.
13. Next, use a large serving plate to cover the top of the pot, upside down. Flip the pot over so the vegetables are now on the serving plate.
14. Reduce the liquid over medium heat by about half. Add 2 tablespoons olive oil and drizzle the liquid over the cooked vegetables. Serve at room temperature.

Chef's note:
This dish can be made with a variety of vegetables of your choice. It's best served at room temperature as a summer dinner appetizer or alone as a light lunch. You can also use butter instead of olive oil in step 14 and serve as a hot accompaniment to meat or fish.

Ingredients: (serves 6)

- 2 medium zucchini
- 300 g green beans, trimmed
- 2 medium aubergines
- 1 large red bell pepper
- 2 large tomatoes
- 1 large whole onion, peeled
- 2 sprigs basil
- ½ cup + 4 tbsp olive oil
- ¼ cup hot water
- 1 tbsp sugar
- 3 tsp salt

Green Beans with Damson Plums and Olive Oil

Changa Restaurant

Preparation:

1. Peel and cube tomatoes.
2. Slice lemon into thin rings.
3. Slice onion into thin rings.
4. Pour half of the olive oil into a pot. Sauté onions and garlic with half of the sugar.
5. Cut off the ends of the green beans, trim them and snap in half. Add to the sauteed onions and season with salt. Add green beans and gently press them down in the pot without stirring. Sprinkle the remaining sugar and pour in lemon juice.
6. Add the cubed tomatoes and press down.
7. Slice the plums in half and remove pit. Place on top of tomatoes, flesh side down.
8. Place lemon slices over mixture and add ½ cup water.
9. Cover the pot and simmer until the beans are tender.
10. Place in serving dish and serve chilled.

Ingredients: (serves 6)

- 1 kg green beans or French beans
- 2 medium yellow onions
- 2 tbsp sugar
- 6 cloves garlic, whole
- 5 medium tomatoes
- 10 damson plums
- ¾ cup olive oil
- 1 lemon
- 1 lemon, juice of

Faux Stuffed Cabbage Stew

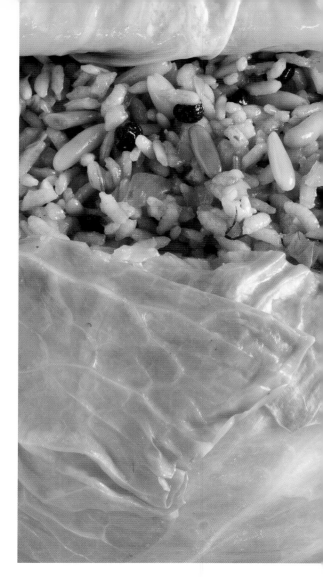

Nevin Halıcı

Preparation:

Preparation of stuffing:
1. Sauté pine nuts in olive oil until light brown.
2. Stir in the onion and sauté until caramelized.
3. Add rice continue to sauté for a few minutes. Add tomato paste and stir.
4. Add spices, sugar, salt and beef stock or water. Cover and bring to the boil. Lower the heat and simmer for about 20 minutes, until all of the liquid is absorbed.
5. Remove from heat and add mint, dill and parsley and stir. Cover and let the mixture rest for 10 minutes.

Preparation of cabbage:
1. Remove the outer leaves.
2. De-core. Create a hollow for stuffing by removing the inner leaves until only about 3-4 leaves are left on the outside.
3. Wash the center of cabbage. Then soak in salted water for 15 minutes, rinse and drain.

Preparation of the stew:
1. Stuff the cabbage with the prepared filling.
2. Cover the stuffed side of the cabbage with some of the extra leaves and place in a pot, stuffed side down. Season with salt and add water and olive oil. Cover and bring to the boil. Then reduce heat and simmer for 40 minutes.
3. When cooked, remove from heat and allow to cool.
4. Drain the liquid from the cabbage. The stuffed sice of the cabbage has to look down. Serve cold.

Ingredients: (serves 6)

Cabbage for stuffing:
- 1 medium cabbage
- 1 cup water
- ¼ cup olive oil
- 2 tsp salt

For soaking the cabbage:
- 5 lt water
- 1 tbsp salt
- A bowl large enough to hold whole cabbage

For the filling:
- 1 cup olive oil
- 1 tbsp pine nuts
- 6 yellow onions, diced
- 2 cups rice
- 1 tbsp tomato paste
- 1 tbsp coriander
- 2 tsp black pepper
- 1 tsp hot paprika
- 1 tsp cinnamon
- 2 tsp sugar
- Salt, to taste
- 1 cup water or beef stock
- 1 cup flat leaf parsley, finely chopped
- 1 cup fresh mint, finely chopped
- 1 cup fresh dill, finely chopped

Artichoke wrapped in Vine Leaves

Istanbul Culinary Institute

Preparation:

Preparation of fava bean filling:
1. Soak dried fava beans overnight
2. Rinse and drain water and place in a pot and add in the diced onion.
3. Add water to cover. Cook until the beans are barely tender, taking care not to overcook.
4. Pour olive oil, stir in dill and season to taste with salt.
5. Remove to a bowl and leave to cool.
6. Divide the bean mixture into six equal parts.

Preparation of artichokes:
1. Chop off about the top third of the artichokes and cut off all but about 5 cm of the stems. Remove the hairy choke.
2. Fill the hollowed inner part of the artichoke with the fava bean mixture.
3. Rinse the brine off the vine leaves. Wrap each artichoke with a whole vine leaf, starting at the bottom and going up to the stem. Leave the stems.
4. Slice the onion, carrot and lemon, and layer them on the bottom of a wide, deep pot. Spread a few layers of vine leaves over the onion, carrot and lemon slices.
5. Arrange the artichokes on top of the vine leaves, with the stems facing up. Season with salt and add water and olive oil.
6. Wet wax paper with water and then drain excess water and place over the artichokes. Simmer on low heat for about 30 minutes or until they are tender enough to pierce easily with a knife.
7. Serve warm or cold.

Ingredients: (serves 6)

- 6 fresh globe artichokes
- 12 vine leaves, plus an additional 10 leaves to line the pot
- 400 ml / 2 cups olive oil
- 1 sheet wax paper
- 1 ½ lemons, juice of
- 1 tbsp salt
- 600 ml / 2 ½ cups water
- 1 medium yellow onion
- 1 medium carrot
- 1 whole lemon

Ingredients for filling:
- 300 g / 2 cups dried fava beans
- 1 medium yellow onion, diced
- Salt, to taste
- 2 tbsp olive oil
- ½ bunch dill, finely chopped

Chef's note:

If you prefer to use fresh fava beans, you don't need to precook them. Lightly sauté thinly sliced onions in a bit of olive oil, then fill the hollowed artichokes with the fresh beans and cooked onions. Wrap with vine leaves as above. Rice pilaf is a good accompaniment to this dish.

Celeriac, Jerusalem Artichoke and Quince Rounds

Vivet Rozales

Preparation:

1. Quarter quinces and celeriac and then cut them in half. With a melon scooper, make rounds and place in a bowl of water with lemon juice to prevent them from discoloring.
2. Peel the Jerusalem artichokes, scoop them into balls and place them in the lemon water.
3. Fill three separate pots with a liter of water each. To each pot, add 2 tbsp flour, the juice of two lemons, 2 tbsp sugar, half a glass of fresh orange juice and 3 tbsp olive oil.
4. Bring the vegetables to the boil in the separate pots, reduce heat to medium, and cook for 15-20 minutes or until fork tender.
5. Use a ladle to transfer quince and Jerusalem artichokeS to the pot with the celeriac. Add 4-5 celery leaves. Cook for an additional 15 minutes.
6. Remove from stove, strain and transfer to a shallow bowl. Garnish with diced red bell pepper and serve.

Ingredients: (serves 6)

- 1 kg celeriac (preferably with leaves)
- 1 kg Jerusalem artichoke
- 1 kg quince
- 6 lemons, juice of
- 6 tbsp flour
- 9 tbsp olive oil
- 6 tbsp sugar
- 1 ½ cups fresh orange juice
- Red bell pepper, diced
- Water

Baba Ghanoush Terrine

Eyüp Kemal Sevinç - Founder, Hobimle Mutluyum Culinary Arts School

Preparation:

1. Cut one of the aubergines into very thin slices.
2. Roast and peel the remaining aubergines. (See pg. 78)
3. Pour olive oil over the thinly cut aubergine slices, season with salt and pepper, and grill on the barbeque or broil.
4. Preheat the oven to 170°C (350°F) and roast the red and yellow bell peppers for 15 minutes.
5. Peel the skins and remove the seeds from roasted peppers.
6. Blanch spinach in boiling salted water for 1 minute, remove and immediately plunge into ice water.
7. Line a terrine mould with stretch wrap. Arrange the grilled aubergine slices so they line the mould. Ensure there are no gaps, since this will be the outer "crust" of your terrine. Reserve enough slices to use as the top layer.
8. Next, layer the aubergine mixture, roasted peppers and spinach in accordance with the effect you would like to create when you slice the terrine.
9. Layer the reserved aubergine slices on top, cover and refrigerate. It's ready for slicing once it is well-chilled.
10. Garnish the Mesclun with thinly sliced red and green peppers. Add sthe juice of a lemon and olive oil and toss.
11. Puree the jarred roast red peppers in a food processor.
12. Mix parsley, chives, basil and virgin olive oil in a blender.
13. Place the terrine on a serving dish. Garnish with the Mesclun salad and red bell pepper puree. Drizzle with virgin olive oil, and serve.

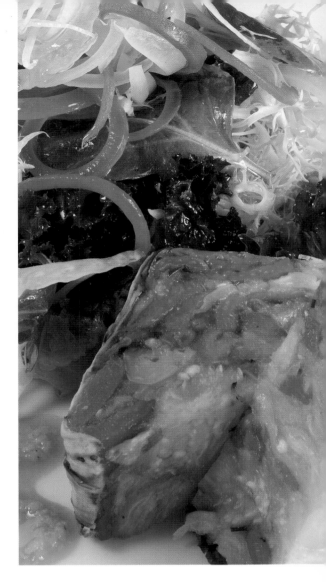

Ingredients: (serves 6)

- 200 g aubergine
- 100 g spinach
- 100 g red bell pepper
- 100 g yellow bell pepper
- 100 g roasted sweet red pepper, from a jar
- 90 g Mesclun
- 1 tbsp virgin olive oil
- 5 g basil
- 5 g flat leaf parsley
- 5 g chives
- 1 tsp salt
- 1 tsp black pepper
- Red and yellow bell peppers, for garnish

Artichoke Soup with Olive Oil

**Maximillian J.W. Thomae - Executive Chef,
Pera Palas Hotel**

Preparation:

1. Sauté the diced onion, artichoke hearts and potato in 1½ tablespoons of olive oil in a medium sized saucepan.
2. Add vermouth and boil until it evaporates.
3. Add chicken stock and saffron and continue boiling until the vegetables are tender. Puree in a food processor.
4. Season with salt and pepper and strain.
5. Drizzle the rest of the olive oil over each dish and serve.

Chef's note:

We suggest a garnish of croutons and/or sliced artichoke hearts in olive oil.

Ingredients: (serves 6)

- 6 globe artichoke hearts
- 1 medium yellow onion, diced
- 1 medium potato, diced

- 30 cl / 1 ⅓ cups Noilly Prat vermouth
- ¼ tsp saffron
- 750 ml / 3 cups chicken stock
- 75 ml / ⅓ cup olive oil
- Salt, to taste
- Black pepper, to taste

Swiss Chard with Chickpeas

Istanbul Culinary Institute

Preparation:

1. Soak chickpeas overnight or for at least 8 hours and drain.
2. Boil the chickpeas in lightly salted water for up to 1 hour, until half-cooked.
3. Heat butter in a pot, add olive oil and onions and sauté
4. When the onions are translucent, stir in the tomato paste. Then add the chickpeas and continue to sauté for a few minutes.
5. Remove the tough stems from Swiss chard. Cut the leaves into long strips and finely chop the tender stems. Add to the pot.
6. Add water and sugar. Season with salt and black pepper. Cook for half an hour or until the chickpeas are tender.
7. Serve warm.

Ingredients: (serves 6)

- 180 g / 1 ½ cups dried chickpeas
- 1 ½ kg large Swiss chard leaves
- 2 medium yellow onions, finely chopped
- 1 ½ tbsp olive oil
- 2 tbsp butter
- 1 ½ tbsp tomato paste
- ½ tsp sugar
- 1 tbsp salt
- 1 tbsp black pepper
- 150 ml / ¾ cup water

Carrots with Rice and Grape Molasses (Pekmez)

Nevin Halıcı

Preparation:

1. Wash and peel the carrots and then cut into bite-size rounds as desired or leave whole if you're using baby carrots and place in a pot.
2. Fill with water to cover and cook covered on medium-low heat for about 30 minutes, or until the carrots are tender.
3. Add butter and rice.
4. Cook for an additional 15-20 minutes; when the rice is tender, stir in the pekmez.
5. Remove from heat after 5-10 minutes.
6. Let it stand for 10 minutes.
7. Place in a serving dish and serve hot.

Chef's note:

This dish can be served as a light main course or as a side dish. Pekmez is a traditional molasses-like syrup usually made from condensed grape juice. It can also be made with figs, mulberry and carob.

Ingredients: (serves 6)

- 750 g carrots
- 600 ml / 2 ⅓ cups water
- 2 ½ tbsp butter
- 3 tbsp rice
- 300 g / 1 ½ cups pekmez (grape molasses) or sugar

Cabbage with Walnuts

Zeynep Çelikkan Kakınç

Preparation:

1. Core the cabbage. Separate the leaves and place in pot of boiling water; cover and cook until tender.
2. Reserve ½ cup of the cabbage stock.
3. Remove cooked cabbage leaves, lightly squeeze off excess liquid and allow to cool. Then cut into bite size pieces.
4. Add diced onions and toss gently with hands until well-mixed.
5. Mix walnuts, garlic, hot paprika and a dash of salt in the blender and add to the cabbage.
6. Mix in yogurt, coriander, mayonnaise, cabbage stock and salt to taste.
7. Place on a serving dish. Garnish with the chopped ends of the spring onions and, if desired, drizzle a little walnut oil over the dish.

Ingredients: (serves 6)

- 2 kg cabbage (600 g can be pickled cabbage)
- 300 g shelled walnuts
- ½ cup cabbage stock
- 2 bulbs of garlic, peeled
- 1 large yellow onion, diced
- 1 medium yellow onion, diced
- 3 tbsp coriander
- 3 tbsp hot paprika
- 6 tbsp mayonnaise
- 400 g / 2 cups strained yogurt
- 1 bunch spring onions (scallions)
- Salt, to taste

Zucchini and Aubergine au Gratin

Gökçen Adar

Preparation:

1. Slice aubergines in half lengthwise, leaving stems intact.
2. Use the sharp tip of a knife to make a slit 5-6mm deep all around the edge of the inside of each, 5mm from the skin.
3. Score the flesh of the aubergine in a cross-hatched pattern 5-6mm deep.
4. Rub salt on the cross-hatched flesh and place flesh side down on the counter for 20-25 minutes or until the dark, bitter juices are drawn out.
5. While the aubergines are draining, grate and salt the zucchini. Let stand for 15-20 minutes.
6. Pre-heat oven to 200°C (400°F). When the dark liquid has drained from the aubergines, place them scored side down on a greased baking dish.
7. Bake the aubergines until easily pierced with a knife, yet still firm and remove from oven.
8. Heat a large frying pan on high heat and add 75ml olive oil.
9. Squeeze the excess liquid from zucchini and cook in the hot olive oil, stirring continuously, until cooked.
10. Season with salt and black pepper, making sure to add salt gradually as the aubergines and zucchini retain some salt. Turn off the heat and allow to cool.
11. Add half of the grated kaşar or provolone cheese, dill, beaten eggs and up to 2 tsp of hot paprika to zucchini.
12. Turn over the baked aubergine halves so the scored side is facing upwards.
13. Sprinkle with salt and drizzle olive oil over the aubergines. Flatten the fleshy portion and then place an equal amount of the zucchini mixture over each one. Place the baking dish back in the oven and remove only when the egg in the zucchini mixture is fully cooked.
14. If desired, sprinkle the remaining cheese and some hot paprika over the aubergines and place back in the oven.
15. After the cheese has melted, remove and serve hot.

Ingredients: (serves 6)

- 3 aubergines
- 6 yellow zucchini
- 250 g / 1 ⅔ cups kaşar or provolone cheese, grated
- 3 - 4 eggs, beaten
- 2 tbsp dill, finely chopped
- 1 tsp black pepper
- 100 ml / ½ cup olive oil
- Salt, to taste
- Hot paprika, to taste

Chef's note:

If desired, sprinkle the remaining cheese and some hot paprika over the aubergines and place back in the oven. After the cheese has melted, remove and serve hot.

Artichoke Salad

Nevin Halıcı

Preparation:

1. Cut off the stems, strip off the leaves and carefully remove the chokes of the artichokes. Rub the artichoke hearts with half a lemon.
2. Put the artichokes hearts in salted boiling water to which you've added a ¼ cup lemon juice.
3. When the artichoke hearts are tender, mash them with a fork and force them through a strainer.
4. Place in a serving dish. Drizzle with a dressing of ¼ cup lemon juice and olive oil. Garnish with black olives.

Chef's note:

Can be served as a dip, a salad or spread on crostini. To make crostini, grill thin slices of baguette bread and drizzle with olive oil.

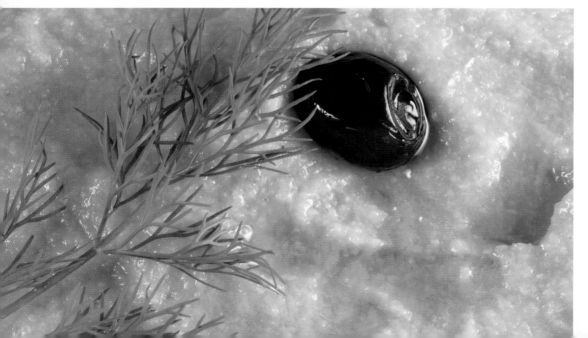

Ingredients: (serves 6)

- 6 globe artichokes
- ½ lemon, to clean artichokes
- 1 tsp salt
- ½ cup lemon juice
- 75 ml / ⅓ cup olive oil
- 6 - 7 black olives

Stuffed Vine Leaves with Cherries

Istanbul Culinary Institute - Fehmi Samancı

Preparation:

1. Soak vine leaves in hot water for at least 6 hours.
2. In a saucepan, roast pine nuts in hot olive oil for 30 seconds.
3. Add chopped onions. Reduce heat and sauté the onions until translucent.
4. Add rice and continue to sauté for another 10-15 minutes. Season with salt and add sugar.
5. Add 100ml boiling water and 150ml cherry juice.
6. Continue cooking until the liquid is absorbed and cool.
7. Add the chopped coriander.
8. Line the bottom of a pot with thin slices of carrot, onion and lemon and cover with a layer of vine leaves.
9. Remove vine leaves for stuffing from the water and snip off their stems.
10. Add a bit of filling to each vine leaf and roll tightly.
11. Arrange the stuffed vine leaves in the pot taking care not to leave any spaces. Then place a layer of cherries on top, then another layer of stuffed vine leaves.
12. Arrange the green plums on the very top and cover with more of the thick vine leaves.
13. Add 50ml water and 200ml cherry juice.
14. In order to keep the stuffed vine leaves intact, place a heatproof plate on top of them. Cover the pot and simmer gently until the liquid is absorbed.

Ingredients: (serves 6)

- 200 g vine leaves
- 10-15 vine leaves, to line pot
- ½ lemon
- ¾ cup olive oil
- 750 g onions, chopped
- 1 onion, sliced
- 1 carrot, sliced
- 250 g rice, rinsed and soaked in water for 20 minutes
- 2 tbsp pine nuts

- 500 g sour cherries, to obtain 350 ml cherry juice
- 6-7 sprigs fresh coriander, leaves only
- 1 tbsp salt, to taste
- Black Pepper, to taste
- 1 tbsp sugar
- ¾ cup water
- 300 g sour green plums

Chef's note:

You may substitute concentrated cherry juice instead of preparing your own with fresh sour cherries.. If you're unable to find cherry juice, place one pitted sour cherry inside of each stuffed vine leaf.

Pureed Peas with Samphire and Fresh Fava Beans

Vivet Rozales

Preparation:

Preparation of Pureed Peas:

1. Boil 2 tablespoons of peas, 1 teaspoon baking soda and 1 teaspoon salt for 15 minutes. Drain and reserve for garnish.

2. Sautee diced onions in olive oil until translucent. Add the remaining peas and sauté for a further 2-3 minutes.

3. Add sugar cubes, 2 teaspoons baking soda and enough water to cover the mixture.

4. Simmer until the peas have absorbed the cooking liquid. Remove from heat and let cool.

5. Put the peas in a food processor.

6. Divide the half bunch of dill in half. Remove the stems and puree the leaves with the peas in the food processor.

7. Use a pastry bag to pipe the pureed peas into rosettes on a serving platter. Decorate each rosette with 2-3 of the reserved whole peas.

8. Place a sprig of dill onto each rosette 10 minutes before serving.

9. Top each rosette with a thin slice of parmesan.

10. If not serving immediately, cover with saran wrap.

Preparation of Samphire:

1. Wash samphire thoroughly and place in pot with enough water to cover. Add ¼ teaspoon baking soda and boil for 15 minutes.

2. Drain the boiled samphire and plunge into cold water. Once chilled, drain.

3. Grasp the end of each stem as you gently strip the edible flesh off the stringy core from end to tip. Be careful not to mash the tender flesh.

4. Put samphire in a bowl of cold water to reduce the salty taste.

5. Remove from the water half an hour before serving and dress with a mixture of fresh lemon juice and virgin olive oil. If desired, add some finely grated garlic to the dressing.

6. Serve as an accompaniment to the pureed peas.

Preparation of Fresh Fava Beans:

1. Boil the shelled fava beans for 5 minutes in 2 cups of water with ¼ teaspoon baking soda until the skins slide off.

2. Drain the beans and remove the skins with your hands.

3. Bring ½ liter water, lemon juice, salt, olive oil and sugar to a boil. Add fava beans and cook for 10-15 minutes. Serve with the pureed peas and samphire.

Ingredients: (serves 6)

Pureed Peas :

- 1 kg fresh peas, shelled
- 1 onion
- 2 cubes sugar
- 3 tsp baking soda
- 60 ml olive oil
- ½ bunch dill
- Parmesan, thinly sliced
- 1 tsp salt

Samphire:

- 1 bunch samphire
- ¼ tsp baking soda
- Lemon juice and olive oil, for dressing
- Garlic, grated, to taste (optional)

Fresh Fava Beans:

- 250 g fava beans, shelled
- 2 tbsp olive oil
- ¼ tsp baking soda
- 1 cube sugar
- 1 lemon, juice of
- 1 tsp salt

Chef's note:

To serve as finger food, cut small fresh apricots in half, remove the pits and hollow out a bit of the flesh. Place some of the pureed peas onto each apricot half and garnish with a sprig of dill. Another alternative is to place some pureed peas on melba toast or spread on crostini.

Deniz börülcesi *is a wild succulent plant that grows in the salt marshes and beaches in the Aegean region and is called samphire or glasswort in English. After cooking, it looks like seaweed but tastes similar to asparagus. This dish can be prepared a day in advance, but be sure to leave the roots intact until after cooking, as it makes it easier to clean off the flesh.*

Baba Ghanoush with Goat Cheese Gratin

Mike Norman

Preparation:

1. Cut goat cheese into wheels and set aside.
2. To prepare baba ghanoush, roast and char aubergines and red bell peppers (see page 78), peel and immediately place in water with lemon juice.
3. Remove from water and in a bowl, lightly blend with tahini, parsley and coriander and season with salt and black pepper.
4. Thinly slice the zucchini and grill on barbeque or broil until crispy.
5. Make a ring mold with the zucchini and fill with the baba ghanoush and top with the pre-cut goat cheese.
6. Place the moulded cheese and aubergine in a hot oven until the cheese melts.
7. Dress the mesclun with lemon and olive oil.
8. Just before serving, drizzle pomegranate molasses around the cheese and rustically arrange mesclun leaves.

Ingredients: (serves 6)

- 120 g goat cheese
- 4 globe aubergines
- 1 tbsp tahini
- 2 zucchini
- 1 red bell pepper
- 2 tbsp / 20 ml pomegranate molasses
- 60 g Mesclun or purslane leaves
- 40 ml / ½ cup mixture of lemon juice and olive oil
- 4 g / ½ tbsp parsley, finely chopped
- 2 g / 1 tsp coriander
- Salt, to taste
- Black Pepper, to taste

Grilled Halloumi Cheese in Vine Leaves

Changa Restaurant

Preparation:

1. Rinse to remove the salt from the cheese.
2. Cut cheese into 14 slices and soak in warm water for 2-3 hours.
3. Wash the vine leaves in warm water. If you're using wine leaves from a jar, soak away the brine in warm water for 4-5 hours. For fresh leaves, blanch in salty water for about 15 seconds.
4. Rinse and pat dry cheese and vine leaves.
5. Place vine leaves on a clean surface and place a slice of cheese in the center of each one. Gather up the edges of each leaf to form a rectangular package.
6. Brush both sides with olive oil.
7. Grill on the barbeque or in a char-grill pan until you see the grill marks on the leaves.
8. Drizzle with chilli sauce and serve immediately before the cheese hardens.

Chef's note:

Halloumi is a traditional Cypriot cheese known in Turkish as "hellim peyniri".

Ingredients: (serves 6)

- 2 packages / 14 slices halloumi cheese
- 14 fresh or jarred vine leaves
- Virgin olive oil
- Sweet chilli sauce

Stuffed Swiss Chard

Şans Restaurant

Preparation:

1. Rinse rice in warm water..
2. Plunge the chard leaves into hot water for 1-2 minutes. Strain excess water.
3. Chop the onions.
4. In a large mixing bowl, mix the chopped onions, ground beef, rice, diced tomato, parsley, dill, dried mint, salt, pepper, hot paprika and cumin and stir. Knead the mixture with your hands until thoroughly mixed.
5. Divide each chard leaf into six, removing thick stem sections.
6. Place a teaspoon of filling on each leaf and roll tightly. Layer as closely as possible in a pot.
7. Add just enough hot water to cover.
8. Add 2 tbsp margarine.
9. Place a heatproof plate, upside down, on top.
10. Cover the pot with a lid and simmer on low heat for 1 hour.
11. Place in a serving dish, garnish with tomatoes and sliced onion and serve hot.

Chef's note:

You can also arrange the stuffed chard on a serving dish and spoon whipped yogurt over the top or simply serve with yogurt on the side.

Ingredients: (serves 6)

- ½ kg large Swiss chard leaves
- 3 yellow onions, minced
- 50 gr / ¼ cup rice
- 300 gr ground beef
- 1 tomato, diced
- ½ bunch flat leaf parsley, finely chopped
- ½ bunch dill, finely chopped
- 2 tbsp margarine
- Salt, to taste
- Black pepper, to taste
- Hot paprika, to taste
- Cumin, to taste
- Dried mint, to taste

Karnıyarık ("Slit Belly" Aubergines)

Istanbul Culinary Institute

Preparation:

1. Peel alternating strips of the aubergine and salt. Rinse after 20 minutes.
2. Fry in sunflower oil until golden brown.
3. Drain the fried aubergines on a paper towel and place in a baking dish.
4. In a saucepan, sauté the chopped lamb meat with finely diced onions and garlic. Add tomato paste, water or beef stock, salt, black pepper, hot paprika, and allspice and stir. Boil for 5 minutes.
5. Add the peeled and finely diced tomatoes, stir and remove from heat.
6. Drain stuffing mixture, reserving the liquid in a separate bowl.
7. Peel, quarter and remove seeds from the tomato you'll be using for garnish. Cut the tips off the banana (yellow wax) peppers, slice in half down the middle and remove seeds. In a saucepan, hit sunflower oil and sauté the tomatoes and peppers. Remove and place on a piece of wax paper.
8. Use a spoon to cut a slit along the length of each aubergine and sprinkle each with a pinch of sugar.
9. Stuff each aubergine with the stuffing mixture. Pour the reserved liquid into a corner of the baking dish.
10. Place a piece of the pre-prepared tomato and peppers on top of each aubergine.
11. Bake in a preheated oven (180°C/350°F) until soft.

Ingredients: (serves 6)

- 600 g, 6 aubergines
- 360 g fatty chopped lamb meat
- 1 medium onion, chopped
- 2 medium tomatoes, peeled and finely diced
- Sunflower oil, sufficient to fry aubergines
- 1 tbsp black pepper
- 1 tbsp hot paprika
- 1 tbsp allspice
- 1 cup water or beef stock
- 2 cloves garlic
- 1 tbsp tomato paste
- 1 tbsp sugar
- Salt, to taste

For garnish:
- 1 tomato
- 2 banana (yellow wax) peppers

Stuffed Quince

Istanbul Culinary Institute

Preparation:

1. Cut off and set aside the tops of the quinces. Remove the core with a paring knife being careful not to pierce the bottom. Place in water with lemon juice to prevent discoloring.
2. Soak the rice in warm water for 20 minutes.
3. In a separate bowl, thoroughly mix the ground beef, onion, garlic, tomatoes, all of the spices and herbs (except the sage), tomato paste and sunflower oil. Then, drain the rice and knead into the mixture with your hands.
4. Divide the filling into 6 equal parts and stuff the quinces, allowing a little room for swelling as the filling cooks. Cover with the tops of the quinces to create a "lid".
5. Place the stuffed quinces in a large baking dish, placing the cinnamon sticks underneath and the sage on top.
6. Pour the vegetable or beef stock over the quinces. Cover with aluminum foil and place in an oven preheated to 170°C (350°F). Bake for 30-35 minutes or until tender. Serve hot.

Ingredients: (serves 6)

- 6 quinces
- 360 g ground beef
- 90 g / ½ cup short-grain rice
- 1 medium onion, chopped
- 2 cloves garlic, finely chopped
- 4-5 sprigs flat leaf parsley, finely chopped
- 4-5 sprigs mint, finely chopped
- 4-5 sprigs dill, finely chopped
- 1 medium tomato, peeled and diced
- 50g / 1 ½ tbsp tomato paste

- 1 tbsp allspice
- 1 tbsp hot pepper flakes
- 1 tbsp hot paprika
- 50 ml / 4 tbsp sunflower oil
- 1lt / 4 cups vegetable or beef stock
- 5 sprigs fresh sage
- 2 cinnamon sticks
- 1 lemon, juice of
- 2 lt / 8 cups water

Stuffed Artichokes with Chopped Meat

Dr. Özge Samancı

Preparation:

1. Cut off the artichoke stems, remove the tough outer leaves and rub with lemon peel.
2. Boil artichokes in salted water for 5 minutes, then submerge in cold water.
3. Use a spoon to fully remove the chokes. Rinse well.
4. For the filling, combine the chopped meat, rice, onion, cinnamon, salt, pepper, mint, parsley and water in a large boil, mixing thoroughly with your hands.
5. Fill each artichoke with the mixture, leaving about 1 cm empty at the top.
6. Place the artichokes in the bottom of a wide pot and fill half way with water. Add butter, cover and bring to the boil.
7. Lower the heat and simmer for about 40 minutes or until the artichokes and the rice are tender.
8. Place on a serving dish and drizzle with the remaining liquid from the pot.

Chef's note:

A modern interpretation of a 19th century Ottoman recipe originally published in the cookbook "Housewife" in 1882. Today, artichokes are still a preferred ingredient in Turkish cuisine.

Ingredients: (serves 6)

- 6 medium globe artichokes
- 2 lemons, halved
- 300 g fatty chopped lamb or mutton
- ¾ cup broken rice
- 250 g onion, chopped
- 10 sprigs mint, finely chopped
- 10 sprigs dill, finely chopped
- 10 sprigs parsley, finely chopped
- 2 ½ tsp cinnamon
- 3 tsp salt
- 3 tsp black pepper
- 3 tbsp water
- 5 tbsp butter

Marmarine

Marianna Yerasimos

Preparation:

1. Remove spinach roots, thoroughly wash the leaves, submerge in boiling water for 3-5 minutes and drain.
2. Place spinach in a greased tray or baking dish. Season with salt and pour melted butter and mix well.
3. Whisk an egg in a small bowl. Add the cheese and season with black pepper and mix. Pour the mixture over the spinach.
4. Bake in a preheated oven at 180˚C/350˚F for 20 minutes or until the cheese has melted and is golden.

Chef's note:

This tasty light cheese dish can also be made with a layer of phyllo pastry on the bottom of the baking dish. You can also add olive oil and garlic, to taste.

Ingredients: (serves 6)

- 1 kg spinach, fresh
- 3 tbsp butter
- 300 g white (feta) cheese
- 3 eggs
- ½ tsp black pepper, freshly ground
- Salt, to taste

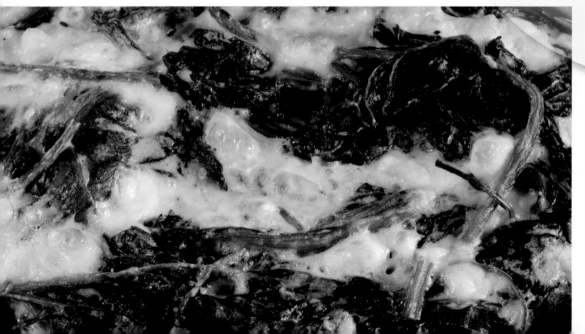

Artichoke with Olive Oil

Beyti Restaurant

Preparation:

1. Clean and prepare the artichokes. (See page 78)
2. Heat olive oil into a pot. Sauté the carrot and shallots for 3-5 minutes. Add flour and continue to sauté for a minute and then add 1 liter hot water.
3. When the carrot and shallots are partially cooked add the diced potato.
4. When the potatoes begin to go tender, take the artichokes out of the lemon water and add to the pot. Add just enough water to cover the artichokes.
5. Add either two lemon halves or the juice of a whole lemon.
6. Bring to a boil, then reduce heat, cover with a piece of wax paper, place the lid on the pot and continue to simmer.
7. When the artichokes are tender place them on a serving dish.
8. Spoon the shallots, carrot and potato into the crevices of the artichoke and allow to cool.
9. Serve chilled.

Ingredients: (serves 6)

- 6 artichokes
- 1 lemon
- 1 medium carrot, sliced
- 1 handful shallots, sliced
- 1 large potato, diced
- ¼ cup olive oil
- 1 tbsp flour
- 1 lt hot water

Carrots with Cardamom and Olive Oil

Changa Restaurant

Preparation:

1. Remove seeds from the cardamom pods and crush with a mortar and pestle or with the flat side of a knife.
2. Peel and finely chop the garlic.
3. Peel the carrots, chop off the ends and peel into long paper-thin strips.
4. Combine the vinegar, water, ground cardamom, sugar, salt and garlic in a large sauce pan. Bring just to the boil, then lower heat and simmer for five minutes.
5. Add carrot strips and olive oil.
6. Cover and bring to the boil once again.
7. Cook for a few minutes and remove from heat.
8. Stir and place into a serving dish. Serve chilled.

Ingredients: (serves 6)

- 7-8 carrots
- ½ cup cider vinegar
- 2 ½ cups water
- 3 cardamom pods
- 2 tbsp sugar
- 1 tsp salt
- 2 cloves garlic, chopped
- 2 cups virgin olive oil

Zucchini au Gratin

İstanbul Culinary Institute - Seray Öztürk

Preparation:

1. Wash and peel zucchini.
2. Pierce each 4-5 times with a toothpick and cook in boiling water for 10 minutes.
3. Cut the unpeeled tomatoes into ½ cm thick slices.
4. Cut the braided cheese into ½ cm thick slices.
5. Peel onions and cut into ½ cm thick rings. Spread the onion rings in a baking dish.
6. Place the thin slices of garlic over the onions. Add olive oil, salt and black peppercorns and toss lightly until the onions are all coated with oil.
7. Remove zucchini from the boiling water. Create a fan shape with each by leaving the top intact and cutting lengthwise slices, equal in thickness, from near the top of the zucchini through to the tail. Ensure that the head of the zucchini remains intact.
8. Place the fan-like zuchini in a baking dish.
9. Spread the sliced tomatoes and cheese among the zucchini.
10. Drizzle with olive oil and bake at 170°C/350°F for 25 minutes.
11. Sprinkle with dill and serve.

Ingredients: (serves 6)

- 6 medium sized zucchini
- 2 large yellow onions
- 2 cloves garlic, thinly sliced
- 3 medium tomatoes, sliced
- 200 g braided cheese
- Black peppercorns, to taste
- Salt, to taste
- Olive oil, to taste
- Dill, chopped

The Basics

To roast aubergines:

Char the aubergines on a grill or in a hot oven for 5-6 minutes, depending on size, turning them until the skin is burned and the flesh is soft. Grasping the stem, used a knife to peel away the blackened skin and discard. Cut off the stem.

Aubergine Puree (Beğendi)

Preparation:

1. Roast the aubergines, as above.
2. Place in a strainer to drain excess liquid.
3. Heat butter, add flour and sauté for 1-2 minutes.
4. Add cold milk and continue stirring until the mixture has thickened.
5. Add aubergines and continue stirring until smooth.
6. Season with salt. Remove from the heat and add grated cheese. Stir and serve.

Ingredients: (serves 6)

- 3 globe aubergines
- 2 tbsp butter
- 250 g cold milk
- 100 g kaşar or provolone cheese, grated
- 1 cup flour
- Salt, to taste

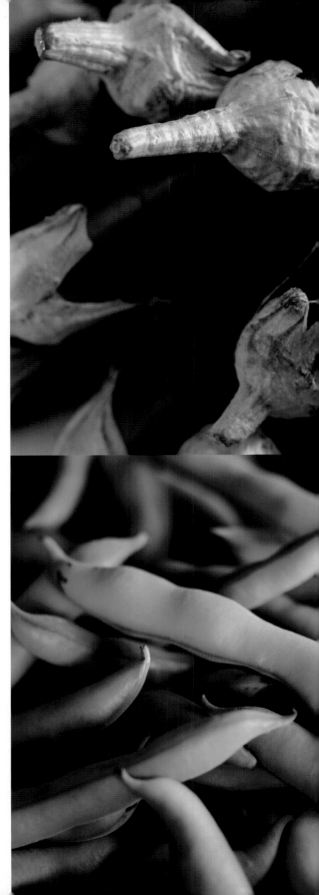

Trimming artichokes:

Pull away the outer leaves. Cut the stalk off at the base. Using a sharp paring knife, cut away and remove the purplish leaves above the heart. Trim away any remaining leaves and tough areas, as though peeling an apple, until the white flesh of the heart emerges. Use the tip of a small spoon to remove all the hairy fibers of the choke. Rub the hearts with salt and lemon to prevent browning. Soak the cleaned artichoke hearts in aciduated water, prepared with 2 tablespoons of lemon juice and 2 tablespoons of flour to one quart of water.

Making vegetable stock:

Preparation:

Roughly chop the vegetables and add to a deep pot of boiling water. Cook on medium heat for 1-1½ hours. Pour through a strainer to remove the cooked vegetables. Reserve the stock.

Ingredients

- 2 lt water / 8 cups water
- 1 celeriac
- 1 carrot
- 1 onion
- 6-7 sprigs parsley
- 8-10 mushroom stems (optional)

Savory

Pastries

Onion Börek

Dr. Özge Samancı

Preparation:

1. Prepare the pastry filling by first melting butter in a large non-stick saucepan. Add onions and sauté on low heat, stirring occassionally, for about 30 minutes or until caramelized.
2. Stir in 1 teaspoon salt and 1½ teaspoons cinnamon and remove from heat.
3. Once it has cooled down, add 3 beaten eggs. Stir and reheat on low heat for 2 minutes.
4. Make the dough by sifting flour and 2 teaspoons salt on a clean counter. Make a little hollow in the flour and gradually mix in ½ cup water. Knead dough until you reach the desired consistency.
5. Divide the dough into 4 and form into balls.
6. Roll out the first ball of dough, about 30cm in size.
7. Mix 2 tablespoons water and 2 tablespoons melted butter which will be used to moisten the dough
8. Grease a 30-cm baking dish with butter and place the first layer of dough on it. Brush it with the water and melted butter mixture.
9. Roll out the second ball of dough and place over the other and spread a layer of the pastry filling and then drizzle water and melted butter.
10. Roll out the third ball of dough and repeat step 9.
11. Roll out the fourth ball of dough and place in the baking dish as the final layer.
12. Brush with beaten egg yolk and with the remaining melted butter and water.
13. Preheat the oven to 180°C/350°F.
14. Bake for 25 minutes until golden brown.

Ingredients: (Serves 6)

For the dough:
- ½ cup water
- 3 cups water
- 2 tsp salt

For the filling:
- 850 g / 5 ⅓ cups white onions, sliced in half moons
- 2 tbsp butter
- 3 eggs, beaten
- 1 tsp salt
- 1 ½ tsp cinnamon

To moisten the dough:
- 2 tbsp water
- 2 tbsp butter, melted

To brush the börek
- 1 egg yolk

Chef's note:

This recipe was adapted from an 18th century anonymous source and includes cinnamon, a popular Ottoman spice.

Sigara Böreği (Cheese Cigars)

Istanbul Culinary Institute

Preparation:

1. Place the sheets of phyllo pastry one on top of the other and cut in half width-wise. Cut each half in half, diagonally. You should now have four piles of triangular phyllo pastry.
2. As you make the cheese cigars, keep the pastry you're not working with from drying by covering it with a damp towel.
3. Make the cheese filling by combining the white cheese (feta), parsley and egg yolk by mashing the mixture in a bowl with a fork.
4. Place about 1 tablespoon of cheese filling at the base of a triangle of phyllo pastry. Wrap the side edges up and over the cheese and roll from the wide end to the tip of the triangle. Repeat until the cheese filling is gone.
5. Seal the ends of the cheese cigars after dipping the edges only in beaten egg.
6. Heat sunflower oil in a deep saucepan and fry until golden brown. Drain any excess oil on a sheet of paper towel.
7. Serve hot or warm.

Ingredients: (For 30 portions)

- 200 g phyllo pastry (4 large sheets)
- 150 g white (feta) cheese
- ½ bunch parsley, finely minced
- 1 egg, beaten
- Sunflower oil, for frying

Gözleme (Swiss Chard Pastry)

Istanbul Culinary Institute

Preparation:

1. Peel and dice tomatoes. Sauté in a little olive oil in a small saucepan. Cook on low heat until the liquid has evaporated and the consistency of the tomato sauce has been reached. Add a little water if it's too thick and season with salt and black pepper.

2. Cut the basil leaves into thin strips. Remove the tomato sauce from the heat and add the basil. Cover and keep warm.

3. Sauté the onions and garlic in butter. Season with salt and black pepper. Add the Swiss chard and continue to sauté until tender. Remove from the heat and allow to cool.

4. Prepare the phyllo pastry. If using round sheets of phyllo pastry, cut off the edges to form a square. Brush each sheet of phyllo with egg white. Fold two of the opposite corners of each sheet of phyllo towards the center, so that the corners meet but don't overlap.

5. Mash the white (feta) cheese in a bowl with a fork and stir in the onion and Swiss chard mixture. Divide this filling into six equal portions.

6. Place 1/6 of the filling in the center of each sheet of phyllo pastry and spread it out in the shape of a square. Brush egg white on the open corners and then fold them towards the center so that they overlap this time. Seal the corners.

7. In a large non-stick saucepan, add enough olive oil to coat the pan and heat. Fry the gözleme one a time, brushing the top with olive oil, and then turning over so that both sides are lightly browned and the cheese filling has melted.

8. Loosely roll each gözleme into a cylinder and cut into 5 equal slices, as you would for a "wrap". Arrange the slices on a plate and serve with the tomato sauce.

Ingredients: (serves 6)

- 600 g Swiss chard, finely chopped
- 140 g / 1 medium onion, finely chopped
- 1 clove garlic, finely grated
- 180 g white (feta) cheese
- 600 g / 2 medium tomatoes, diced
- 3 sprigs basil
- 6 sheets phyllo pastry
- 3 g / 2 tbsp butter
- 2 eggs, whites only
- 20 g / 1 ½ tsp olive oil
- Salt, to taste
- Black Pepper, to taste

Poğaça (Cheese Buns)

Istanbul Culinary Institute - Hande Bozdoğan

Preparation:

1. Mash the white (feta) cheese in a bowl with a fork, or grate.
2. Add black pepper and dill.
3. Mix olive oil and yogurt in a separate shallow bowl.
4. Mix in the salt, baking soda, egg white and flour and knead.
5. Prepare small pieces of dough, forming whatever shape you wish and fill each with the cheese filling.
6. Arrange on a baking tray. Brush with the egg yolk.
7. Sprinkle with black cumin or sesame seeds and bake at 170°C/340°F in a preheated oven for 35-40 minutes or until golden brown.

Chef's note:

Poğaça is a popular breakfast treat in Turkey. It can also be prepared with minced meat, potatoes or other savory fillings.

Ingredients: (serves 6)

For the filling:
- 250 g white (feta) cheese
- Black Pepper, to taste
- 1 tbsp dill, finely chopped

For the dough:
- 1 egg, yolk and white separated
- 1 cup olive oil
- 1 cup yogurt
- 1 tsp baking soda
- 1 tsp salt
- 1 ½ cups flour

Açamuka (Cheese Pastry)

Zeynep Çelikkan Kakınç

Preparation:

1. Shred the cheese length-wise into long, thick strips.
2. Boil a pot of water and add salt and butter, then the cornmeal, stirring constantly.
3. Continue cooking until the smell of the cornmeal is gone.
4. When the water has absorbed, but the mixture is still moist and sticky, gradually add the cheese, stirring constantly.
5. When the cornmeal and cheese are thoroughly combined, remove from the heat and place on a serving dish.
6. If desired, create a hollow in the middle and add some melted butter.
7. Serve hot.

Ingredients: (serves 6)

- 7 ½ cups water
- 4 ½ cups cornmeal
- 3 tbsp butter
- 750 g Çerkez cheese (or string cheese)
- Salt, to taste

Pumpkin Fritters

Istanbul Culinary Institute

Preparation:

1. Peel, remove the seeds and grate the pumpkin; peel and finely grate the fresh ginger.
2. In a large mixing bowl, combine the grated pumpkin, ginger, spring onions, flour, eggs, mineral water, 5 ml olive oil, and a dash each of salt and black pepper. The mixture should have the consistency of porridge.
3. Preheat a non-stick saucepan on medium heat. Add enough oil olive to coat the pan.
4. Use a ladle or large serving spoon to put just enough of the mixture into the saucepan to make one fritter, ensuring that it covers the bottom of the pan evenly. Fry until golden brown on both sides. Keep the cooked fritters warm on a plate until all of the fritters are fried.
5. Divide each fritter into four pieces, place on a serving dish and serve warm.

Ingredients: (serves 6)

- 1.5 kg pumpkin, roughly grated
- 10 g / 2 tablespoons fresh ginger, finely grated
- ½ bunch spring onions (scallions), finely chopped
- ¼ bunch dill, finely chopped
- 30 g / 1 ½ tbsp flour
- 2 eggs
- 100 ml / ½ cup mineral water
- 5 ml / 1 ½ tsp olive oil
- 15 ml / 4 ½ tsp olive oil (for frying)
- Salt, to taste
- Black Pepper, to taste

Egg Noodles with Goat Cheese and Walnuts

Istanbul Culinary Institute

Preparation:

1. Sift flour on a clean counter. Create a hollow in the middle of the flour. Into it, add the eggs and season with salt. Gradually knead in the water to form a firm dough.

2. Divide the dough into 4, cover with a damp towel and let sit for half an hour.

3. Roll out each ball of dough to the thickness of an egg noodle and let it dry.

4. Using a knife, cut the rolled-out dough into thin strips. Place the strips on top of each other and cut into thinner strips. Sprinkle with a little flour and spread out on a tray. Dry the noodles in the sun for 12 hours or in the oven at 100°C/210°F for 20-25 minutes.

5. Bring a large pot of water to the boil and season with salt. Add the noodles and cook until tender and drain.

6. Melt butter in a saucepan and add the walnuts. Sauté for 1-2 minutes and then add the noodles. Sauté for an additional 4-5 minutes. Stir in the crumbled goat cheese and serve hot.

Ingredients: (serves 6)

- 3 cups flour
- 2 eggs
- 50 ml / ¼ cup water
- 1 tbsp salt
- ½ cup water, for the dough
- 4 tbsp butter
- ½ cup shelled walnuts
- 50 g / ½ cup hard goat cheese, crumbled

Rices

Tomato Pilaf

Istanbul Culinary Institute

Preparation:

1. Soak rice in lightly salted water for 20-30 minutes.
2. Rinse the rice in a sifter until the water runs clear.
3. Heat the chicken stock in a pot.
4. Core the stem of the tomatoes and lightly cut an "X" at the base. Bring water to the boil in a separate pot. Fill a deep bowl with ice water. Plunge the tomatoes into the boiling water for 30 seconds and then immediately into the ice water.
5. Remove the tomatoes from the ice water and peel the skins. Cut the tomatoes in half and then cut in half again. Gently squeeze out the seeds and juices.
6. Put sunflower oil and butter in the pan you will use to make the pilaf. Add the rice and lightly sauté for a few minutes, stirring occasionally. Add tomato paste and continue to sauté for 1-2 minutes before adding the tomatoes.
7. Add the preheated chicken broth and season with salt and black pepper. Cook covered on medium heat.
8. When the liquid has absorbed, reduce heat to low and place a gauze or cotton cloth between the lid and pot. Simmer gently for about 8 minutes and turn off the heat. Keep the pilaf covered and allow it to steam for 20 minutes before serving.

Ingredients: (serves 6)

- 480 g / 3 cups short grain rice
- 500 ml / 2 ½ cups chicken stock
- ½ kg / 5 ripe medium tomatoes
- 2 tbsp butter
- 1 ½ tbsp sunflower oil
- 1 ½ tbsp tomato paste
- Salt, to taste
- Black Pepper, to taste

Chicken and Almond Pilaf

Istanbul Culinary Institute

Preparation:

1. Bring vegetable or chicken stock to the boil in a saucepan.
2. Melt butter and sunflower oil in a separate suacepan. Stir in, in order, the almonds, carrot, rice, thyme, hot paprika, mint and chicken.
3. Add spring onions and season with salt. Add stock, stir and simmer covered on medium-low heat.
4. When all of the liquid has absorbed, reduce heat to low for 8 minutes, and then remove from heat.
5. Allow the rice to continue steaming, covered, for an additional 20 minutes, then serve.

Ingredients: (serves 6)

- 480 g / 2 ½ cups rice
- 240 g skinless chicken breast, cut into matchstick strips
- 50 g / ½ cup almonds, peeled
- 1 medium carrot, julienned
- 3 spring onions (scallions)
- 500 ml / 2 cups vegetable or chicken stock
- 1 tbsp dried mint
- 1 tbsp dried thyme
- 2 tsp hot paprika
- 2 tbsp butter
- 2 tbsp sunflower oil
- Salt, to taste
- Black Pepper, to taste

Bulgur Pilaf with Chestnuts

Asitane Restaurant

Preparation:

1. Cut an "X" into one side of the chestnuts. Boil in salted water for up to 10 minutes. Shell and halve the chestnuts.
2. Slice the halved onions horizontally to create half moon-shaped pieces.
3. Make sure that the bulgur and raisins are free of stems and foreign objects.
4. In a heavy saucepan, cook onions in 3 tablespoons of butter over moderate heat, stirring occassionally until golden brown, 5 -7 minutes.
5. Add beef stock, remaining butter, raisins, cumin, allspice and sea salt and bring to a boil.
6. Add the chestnuts and bulgur. Cook on high heat for 3-4 minutes; reduce heat to low and simmer for an additional 10-15 minutes until all the liquid has absorbed.
7. Remove from heat and stir only after it has rested for 15 minutes.
8. Spoon onto a serviing dish, sprinkle with dill and serve.

Ingredients: (serves 6)

- 3 cups coarse bulgur
- 6 cups beef stock
- 300 g whole chestnuts
- 2 small red onions, chopped
- 8 tbsp butter
- 100 g / ½ cup small, plump raisins
- 2 tsp cumin
- 1 tsp allspice
- 1 bunch dill, finely chopped
- Sea salt, to taste

Vegetable Bulgur Pilaf

Deniz Alphan

Preparation:

1. In a heavy saucepan, cook onions in olive oil over moderate heat, stirring occassionally until golden brown, 5 -7 minutes.
2. Cut the red bell and banana peppers into ¾ inch squares and sauté for a few minutes with the onions.
3. Add water. Bring to a boil and then add the bulgur.
4. Add the spices and reduce heat to low.
5. When all the liquid has absorbed, add dollops of butter and turn off heat.
6. Add spring onions and carrots. They'll cook as the bulgur continues to steam.
7. Add dill and serve hot.

Ingredients: (serves 6)

- 2 cups coarse bulgur
- 2 ½ cups water
- 1 medium yellow onion, chopped
- 1 bunch spring onions (scallions), finely chopped
- 1 bunch dill, finely chopped
- 1 medium carrot, grated
- 2 medium red bell peppers
- 2 medium banana (yellow wax) peppers
- ½ teaspoon black pepper
- ½ teaspoon allspice
- 3 tbsp butter
- 100 ml / ½ cup olive oil
- Salt, to taste

Herbed Lamb Pilaf

Hülya Ekşigil

Preparation:

1. Fill a large bowl with hot water, add a generous pinch of salt and the rice. Stir once or twice and let to rest.
2. Heat olive oil in a cast-iron saucepan. Add lamb and brown on high heat, stirring frequently.
3. Cut the apple in half and removed seeds. Insert two cloves into each half.
4. Add the apples to the lamb, pour in lemon juice, reduce heat to low and simmer until the lamb juices are completely reduced.
5. Meanwhile, finely chop the spring onions. When the lamb juices have evaporated, remove the apples and stir in ½ teaspoon salt and chopped onions and turn off the heat.
6. Rinse the rice until all of the starch is gone and the water runs clear. Pour ¼ cup vegetable oil into a large pot and sauté the rice.
7. Meanwhile, add 1 tablespoon salt to 2½ cups of boiling water.
8. Pour the boiling water into the pot with the lightly browned rice. Cook on high heat until the rice absorbs the water, and then reduce heat to low.
9. Finely chop the herbs. When the rice is fully cooked, add the meat, herbs and spices, and stir thoroughly. Turn off the heat.
10. Place a double folded gauze or cotton cloth between the lid and the pot and close securely. After the pilaf has steamed for an additional 15-20 minutes, serve with a green salad.

Ingredients: (serves 6)

- 500 g lamb (trimmed and cubed)
- 1 large red apple
- ½ lemon, juiced
- 4 whole cloves
- 2 cups short grain rice
- ¼ cup vegetable oil
- 2 tbsp olive oil
- 2 ½ cups boiling water
- 1 bunch spring onions (scallions), finely minced chopped

- 1 small bunch mint, finely chopped
- 1 bunch flat leaf parsley, finely minced
- 1 bunch dill, finely minced
- 1 ½ tsp black pepper
- 1 ½ tsp cumin
- 1 ½ tsp allspice
- 1 ½ tsp cinnamon
- 1 ½ tsp salt

Chef's note:

A feast in itself, this pilaf dish is best with a side of green salad with olive oil and lemon dressing. For a fresh, light contrast to the pilaf, avoid superfluous salad ingredients. We recommend bibb, cos or romaine lettuce, perhaps mixed with arugula (rocket) and fresh herbs such as dill.

Notes

Seafood

Pan-Fried Zander

Asitane Restaurant

Preparation:

1. Filet the zander into six portions being careful to remove the tiny bones.
2. Pound each filet, about 5mm thick.
3. Mix chopped dill, onions and spices.
4. Season the mixture with sea salt.
5. Slice each filet in half width-wise. Spoon an equal amount of the mixture on the bottom half of the filet. On top of the mixture, place a slice of skinless lemon.
6. Fold each filet in half, curling the edges to seal.
7. Lightly coat the filets with flour. Heat olive oil in a non-stick frying pan pan and cook on each side until golden.
8. Garnish with arugula (rocket) and lemon and serve.

Ingredients: (serves 6)

- 1.8 kg zander, six 300 g filets
- 3 yellow onions, chopped
- 2 lemons, skinless and sliced
- 12 peppercorns
- 2 tsp hot paprika
- 6 bay leaves
- 750 ml / 3 ½ cups olive oil
- 1 bunch dill, finely chopped
- Sea salt, to taste
- 2 tbsp sumac
- 300 g / 2 ½ cups flour

Baked Crispy Sardines

İnci Birsel

Preparation:

1. Preheat the oven to 180°C/350°C.
2. Rinse and pat dry sardines and rub with salt and black pepper. Arrange the sardines in a single layer on the bottom of greased baking dish, with their tails facing the center of the dish.
3. Whisk lemon juice, white wine and olive oil and pour over the fish.
4. In a mixing bowl, use a fork to mix the lemon peel, garlic, parsley and bread crumbs. Spread this mixture evenly over the sardines.
5. Drizzle 1-2 tablespoons of olive oil over the sardines.
6. Place the baking dish in the center of the preheated oven and bake for 30-40 minutes, until the fish is done and the bread mixture crispy.
7. Serve with a glass of white wine.

Ingredients: (serves 6)

- 1,5 kg fresh sardines or anchovies, scaled, gutted and heads removed
- 6 cloves garlic, finely chopped
- 1 handful flat leaf parsley, finely chopped
- 1 large lemon, zest and juice of
- ½ cup white wine
- ½ cup olive oil
- 1 cup bread crumbs, from day old bread
- Salt, to taste
- Black Pepper, to taste

Poached Sea Bass

Kıyı Restaurant's

Preparation:

1. Melt butter in a large frying pan and sauté the tomatoes, onions, mushrooms, banana (yellow wax) peppers, peppercorns, parsley and white wine.
2. When the vegetables are tender, place the sea bass on top of the vegetables, add 1 cup of water and cook for 5 minutes.
3. Remove the fish and place on a baking tray.
4. Add and stir in the cream to the vegetables and mix thoroughly. Then pour the mixture over the fish.
5. Sprinkle the grated cheese over the top.
6. Bake in a preheated oven at 200°C/390°F for 20 minutes.

Ingredients: (serves 6)

- 1 kg sea bass filets
- 350 g / 2 ½ cups tomatoes, diced
- 50 g / ⅓ cup onions, diced
- 50 gr / 3 tbsp butter
- 100 g / ⅔ cup mushrooms, thinly sliced
- 50 g / ½ cup kaşar or provolone cheese, grated
- 2 banana (yellow wax) peppers
- ¼ bunch flat leaf parsley, chopped
- 2 tbsp cream
- 4-5 peppercorns
- 1 cup water
- 75 ml / ⅓ cup white wine

Anchovy Croquettes

Mike Norman

Preparation:

1. Mix flour, baking soda, sugar and salt in a deep bowl. Add the melted butter and milk and mix lightly to incorporate all ingredients.
2. Fold in the beaten egg white and add chopped dill.
3. Place a fresh anchovy filet in a hot non-stick frying pan and top with a generous spoonful of the mix.
4. Fry on both sides and make sure they are cooked through.
5. Repeat steps 3-4 for each fish.
6. Garnish with greens and slices of fresh lemon. Serve warm.

Ingredients: (serves 6)

- 12 fresh anchovies, fileted
- 110 g / 1 cup + 1 tbsp flour
- 150 ml / $^2/_3$ cup milk
- 5 g / 1 tsp baking soda
- 3 g / 2 tsp sugar
- ½ tsp salt
- 60 g / 4 tbsp butter, melted
- 1 egg white, beaten
- 1 bunch dill, chopped

Stuffed Mussels with Saffron

Istanbul Culinary Institute

Preparation:

1. Remove stems and foreign matter from the currants and rice. Rinse separately and reserve.
2. Soak a pinch of saffron in hot vegetable stock (See page79) or hot water for 10-15 minutes.
3. Heat olive oil in a large, wide saucepan. Add and sauté pine nuts until golden brown and then add the onions.
4. When the onions have caramelized add the rice and continue to sauté.
5. After 6-7 minutes, add, in order, the currants, salt, sugar, and saffron infused vegetable stock. Simmer until the rice has absorbed the cooking liquid.
6. Remove from heat, add black pepper, allspice, cinnamon, mint, dill, parsely and sugar. Stir and allow to stand until all of the flavors are blended.
7. Stuff the mussels with above filling, leaving no empty space, but without over stuffing.
8. Layer the stuffed mussels in a large saucepan and add 250 ml water.
9. Weigh down the mussels by placing a heatproof plate on top. Simmer on low heat for 20-25 minutes.
10. Once stuffed mussels have cooled, remove from pan one at a time and arrange on a large serving dish or tray. Serve with wedges of lemon.

Chef's note:

Stuffed mussels are more flavorful after they have been refrigerated for a day.

Ingredients: (serves 6)

- 24 medium mussels, rinsed, trimmed and scrubbed
- 180 g / 1 cup rice, soaked
- 1 heaping tbsp pine nuts
- 1 tbsp black pepper
- 1 tbsp allspice
- 25 g / 4 tbsp currants, soaked
- 1 tbsp cinnamon
- ¼ bunch mint, finely chopped
- ¼ bunch dill, finely chopped
- 2 medium onions, finely chopped
- ¼ bunch flat leaf parsley
- 1 tbsp sugar
- 125 ml / ½ cup olive oil
- 125 ml / ½ cup hot water or vegetable stock
- Salt, to taste
- 1 pinch saffron
- 250 ml / 1 cup water
- 2 lemons, wedges

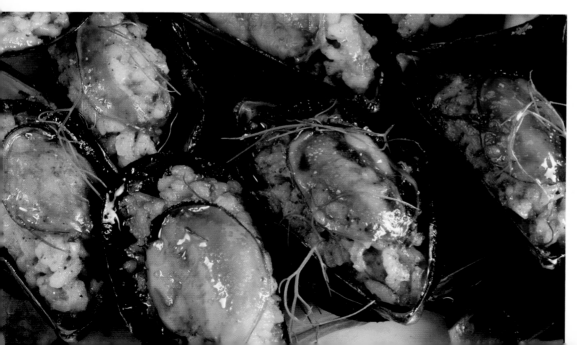

Tiryaki Sauce

Istanbul Culinary Institute - Bülent Metin

Preparation:

1. Combine all of the ingredients, except for the corn starch and coriander in a sufficiently large saucepan.
2. Bring to a boil on high heat, then lower the heat and gently simmer for 20 minutes, stirring occasionally.
3. Mix corn starch with about 10 ml of water, stir and then slowly add to the simmering sauce until you reach the desired consistency.
4. Add the finely chopped fresh coriander to sauce and remove from heat.

Chef's note:

Tiryaki sauce can be served with any grilled fish or vegetable. If rakı is unavailable, Pernod or pastis can be substituted.

Ingredients: (serves 6)

- 200 g / 1 cup brown sugar
- 100 ml / ½ cup rakı
- 240 ml / 1 cup soy sauce
- 250 ml / 1 cup orange juice
- 2 hot red chilli peppers, finely chopped
- 5 hot green peppers, finely chopped
- 25 g fresh ginger root, finely chopped
- 75 g / 5 tbsp blossom honey
- 10 g / 1 ½ tbsp corn starch
- 2 cloves garlic, grated
- 1 package fresh coriander, tough stems removed

Sea Bass in Milk Sauce with Vegetable Mashed Potatoes

Gökçen Adar

Preparation:

1. Cut the onions into thin slices. Cook onions in 2 tablespoons of olive oil in a heavy skillet over medium heat.
2. Wash the Swiss chard leaves and cut into small pieces. Add to the onions.
3. In a separate pot, boil the potatoes until tender, then peel and mash.
4. Grill the red bell pepper in the broiler. Remove the stem, dice and add to the mashed potatoes.
5. Add the sautéed onions and Swiss chard to the mashed potatoes and mix.
6. Coat the fish filets with flour. Heat olive oil in a large frying pan. Fry the filets on both sides.
7. Then squeeze the juice of half a lemon on the fish and pour half of the milk over it.
8. Add the chopped dill and capers. Put the lid on the frying pan and turn off the heat. Wait for one minute and then remove the fish.
9. Repeat steps 6-8 for the remaining fish filets.
10. To serve, place a serving of vegetable mashed potatoes on a dish, place the sea bass on top and garnish with chopped dill and capers.

Ingredients: (serves 6)

- 6 sea bass filets
- 1 lemon, juice of
- 600 ml / 3 cups milk
- 150 g / 1 ¼ cup flour
- 1 bunch dill, finely chopped
- 3 ½ tbsp capers
- Salt, to taste

For the mashed potatoes:
- 4 medium potatoes
- 8 Swiss chard, leaves only
- 2 medium onions
- 2 tbsp olive oil
- Olive oil, as needed for frying
- 1 red bell pepper, grilled

Stewed Octopus with Mastic

Gökçen Adar

Preparation:

1. Place the well pounded or frozen octopus in a pot. Add wine and a diced onion. Cover and simmer, without adding salt, for about 2 hours or until tender and easy to pierce with a knife.

2. Soak the shallots in boiling water for 10 minutes. Peel skins, but leave the roots intact so the shallots don't come apart.

3. Peel the garlic and separate cloves.

4. Heat a large saucepan on medium heat and add olive oil.

5. Sauté shallots and garlic cloves in batches until they are tender but still retain their shape. Use a slotted spoon to remove each batch as it is cooked, draining the oil back into the pan as you do so.

6. Remove the octopus from the pot.

7. In a separate saucepan, simmer the shallots, sliced garlic cloves, crushed mastic, rosemary, cinnamon, salt, lemon or orange peel and 1 cup of the stock from the octopus until the mixture reaches the consistency of a sauce.

8. Pour the sauce over the octopus and serve hot.

Chef's note:

The mastic shrub or small tree is found throughout the Mediterranean region. Drops of mastic gum are harvested from the resin "weeping" out of cuts in the bark of the tree. It is used as a spice to give foods a distinctive aroma and flavor. In Turkey, mastic is usually used to flavor milk puddings.

Ingredients: (serves 6)

- 1.5 kg octopus
- 750 g shallots
- 1 bulb garlic
- 1 sprig rosemary
- 1 lemon or small orange, peel of, cut into matchsticks
- 2 tbsp lemon juice
- 2 drops of mastic resin, crushed
- ½ tsp cinnamon
- 200 ml / 1 cup red or white wine
- 150 ml / ¾ cup olive oil
- 1 tsp salt

Swiss Chard Stuffed with Seafood

Istanbul Culinary Institute

Preparation:

1. Soak the rice in a bowl of warm water for 30 minutes. Drain and rinse repeatedly until the water runs clear.

2. Add 5 grams of salt to a large pot of boiling water. Blanch the Swiss chard leaves for 10-15 seconds, then place on a paper towel and pat dry.

3. Using a sharp knife, trim away the Swiss chards stems, including the bottom of the thick center rib, taking care not to damage the leaves. Use the handle of the knife to crush the tough rib extending from the bottom of the leaf to the center of the leaf.

4. Bring water or vegetable stock (See page 79) to a boil in a small saucepan.

5. Heat olive oil in a frying pan and sauté the onions. When they're tender and have begun to caramelize, add the rice and continue to sauté. When the rice is translucent, add the seafood. Then add black olives and continue to sauté. Add 100 ml of the hot water or vegetable stock. Season with salt and black pepper. When the rice is half cooked, remove from the heat and stir in the fresh herbs.

6. Set the filling aside to cool. Preheat oven to 160°C/320°F.

7. Stuff the Swiss chard as follows: Place a leaf on a flat surface with the stem end facing you. Place 1 tablespoon of filling near the stem. Fold the stem end over the filling, and then fold both sides inward. Now roll tightly from end to tip, so none of the filling will spill out. Arrange the stuffed leaves in a baking dish.

8. Add 150 ml of water or vegetable stock and 50 ml of fish sauce to the baking dish. Cover with aluminium foil and bake in a preheated oven for 30 minutes.

9. Serve hot.

Ingredients: (serves 6)

- 1.2 kg / 1 large bunch Swiss chard
- 90 g / ½ cup rice
- 3 medium onions, cut into thin half moons
- 2 medium calamari tubes, cubed
- 1 filet of sea bass, cubed
- ½ cup baby shrimp

- ⅕ large filet of salmon, cubed
- 150 ml + 100 ml / 1 cup water or vegetable stock
- 10 g / 1 ½ tsp salt
- 10 g / 1 ½ tsp pepper
- ¼ bunch fresh dill, chopped
- ¼ bunch fresh mint, chopped

- 125 ml / ½ cup olive oil
- 12 black olives, pitted and chopped
- 50 ml / 3 ½ tbsp fish sauce

Octopus Carpaccio with Daikon and Celery

Sunset Grill & Bar

Preparation:

1. Cut the tentacles of the octopus, discard head and rinse.
2. Combine the stock ingredients in a large pot. Add the octopus and bring to a boil. Simmer covered and cook for 1 hour.
3. Remove from heat and cool for 30 minutes.
4. Cut the boiled octopus into thin slices.
5. Cut the daikon and celery stalk into slices. Place the slices on a platter with the octopus.
6. Combine the ingredients for the sauce.
7. Season the octopus with salt and black pepper, pour in sauce and toss.
8. Garnish with fresh herbs and serve.

Ingredients: (serves 6)

For the stock:
- 500 g octopus
- 3 lt water
- 15 cl / ⅔ cup red wine
- 100 ml / ½ cup soy sauce
- 150 g / ¾ cup sugar

For the sauce:
- 150 ml / ¾ cup olive oil
- 40 ml / 3 tbsp lemon juice
- 80 ml / ⅓ cup soy sauce
- 5 g / 1 tsp freshly ground black pepper

For the main dish:
- 360 g boiled octopus
- 120 g daikon
- 60 g / ½ cup boiled celery stalk
- 5 g / 1 tsp sea salt
- 10 g / 2 tsp freshly ground black pepper
- 20 g / 2 tsp fresh herbs, as garnish

Baked Filet of Grouper with Vegetable Croquettes & Roasted Pepper Cream Sauce

Ümit Yüksel - Sheraton Istanbul Maslak Hotel

Preparation:

1. Have your fishmonger divide the grouper into 6, 220 g portions and keep the bones.

2. Marinate the fish for at least 2 hours or at most 1 day in a marinade of the finely chopped basil, 2 tablespoons olive oil, salt and black pepper.

3. Sear the fish for 1-2 minutes on both sides in a non-stick saucepan over medium-high heat. Transfer to a baking tray.

4. On a separate tray, crumble 6 slices of stale bread.

5. Melt 1 tablespoon butter in a saucepan and sauté the garlic and drizzle this mixture over the bread crumbs.

6. Sprinkle the bread crumbs over the fish and bake for 7-8 minutes at 180°C/350°F, making certain the fish doesn't dry out.

7. Peel and roughly grate the carrot and zucchini and place in a bowl. Stir in 2 tablespoons flour, 1 egg, finely chopped coriander and season with salt and black pepper.

8. Use a mould in the size of your choosing and fry six equal portions of the vegetable mixture, on both sides, until golden brown.

9. Place the red bell pepper under the broiler and roast.

10. Soak the bones left over from the fish filet in cold water for 15-20 minutes and drain.

11. Fill a small pot with water. Add the scraps from the vegetables and herbs (peels and stems) and the fish bones. Boil for 20 minutes to make a fish stock. Remove from heat and cool.

12. In a separate saucepan, heat 1 tablespoon olive oil and melt 1 tablespoon butter. Add 2 tablespoons flour and sauté for 3-4 minutes. Add sufficient cooled fish stock and ⅓ cup cream to make a cream sauce.

13. Add the diced roasted red bell pepper to the cream sauce and season with salt and black pepper. Simmer for 6-7 minutes. Then, puree the sauce in a blender or food processor.

14. Plate the vegetable croquettes and baked fish and top with hot cream sauce.

Ingredients: (serves 6)

- 1.3 kg grouper, filets
- Salt, to taste
- Black Pepper, to taste
- ½ package fresh basil, chopped
- 1-2 cloves garlic, grated
- 6 slices stale white bread, crusts removed
- 100 g / ⅓ cup cream
- 30 g / 1 red bell pepper, roasted
- ½ package fresh coriander, chopped
- 150 g zucchini, roughly grated
- 150 g carrot, roughly grated
- 3 tbsp olive oil
- 30 g / 2 tbsp butter
- 1 egg
- 4 tbsp flour

Stuffed Calamari

Changa Restaurant

Preparation:

1. Clean and rinse the squid so the body resembles an open cylinder.
2. Finely chop the sun-dried tomatoes.
3. Crumble the cheese and stir together with thyme, tomatoes and olive oil. Season with salt and black pepper.
4. Gently stuff the squid with the cheese filling and weave with a toothpick horizontally across wide opening of each squid to seal. Cook on a grill pan until you can see grill marks and the cheese filling has melted.
5. Remove toothpicks, garnish with chives and serve.

Chef's note:

Tulum cheese is a semi-hard, aged cheese matured in a goat hide. The taste and texture are unlike that of regular goat cheese, so the best substitute is white (feta) cheese.

Ingredients: (serves 6)

- 12 whole small squid
- 300 g tulum or white (feta) cheese
- 100 g sun-dried tomatoes, finely chopped
- 4 tsp thyme leaves
- 3 tbsp olive oil
- 1 tbsp chives, chopped
- Salt, to taste
- Black Pepper, to taste

Spicy Calamari with Pickled Turnips

Aret Sahakyan

Preparation:

1. Cut the turnip into strips 1cm x 4 cm.
2. Put salt and water in a pot and stir to dissolve. Add white wine vinegar and bring to a boil.
3. Place the turnip strips, cubed beetroot and spices inside a sterilized jar.
4. Add enough boiling vinegar water to cover and allow it to cool.
5. When cool, cover with wax paper and seal the lid tightly.
6. Wait three days for the vegetables to pickle. If left unopened, they will keep for up to 4 months. Once opened, refrigerate.
7. To make the spicy paste, grind the cumin seed, coriander seeds and peppercorns using a mortar and pestle.
8. Heat the olive oil in a small saucepan and sauté the garlic until soft. Add it to the ground spices, along with salt, and continue pounding until the mixture reaches the consistency of a smooth paste.
9. Stir in the lemon zest and the finely chopped thyme.
10. Score the inside of the calamari with a cross-hatch pattern, then rub all over with the spicy paste.
11. Heat the grill, brush it with olive oil and place the calamari in the hottest part, scored side down. Cook for 2 minutes and remove from heat.
12. Toss the warm, boiled beans with the lemon juice, rosemary and olive oil. Season with salt and black pepper.
13. Divide the beans among the plates and arrange the calamari on top. Garnish with the pickled turnip strips on the side.

Ingredients: (serves 6)

Ingredients for the Calamari:

- 12 squid, cleaned tubes of
- ½ cup fresh cranberry beans, boiled
- ¼ cup extra virgin olive oil
- ½ lemon, juice of
- 2 sprigs fresh rosemary, finely chopped
- Salt, to taste
- Black Pepper, to taste

Ingredients for the spicy paste:

- 1 tbsp cumin seeds
- 1 tbsp coriander seeds
- 1 tbsp white peppercorns
- 30 ml / 1 tbsp extra virgin olive oil
- 3 cloves garlic, chopped
- ½ tsp sea salt
- 1 lemon, grated rind of
- 1 tbsp thyme sprig, chopped

Ingredients for the Pickled Turnips:

- 4 turnips, peeled
- 850 ml / 3 ½ cups water
- 60 g / ¼ cup sea salt
- 300 ml / 1 ¼ cup white wine vinegar
- 1 small beetroot, rinsed and cubed
- 4 sprigs thyme, chopped
- 10 black peppercorns
- 3 bay leaves

Chilled Sardines with Lemon Zest and Currants

Changa Restaurant

Preparation:

1. Cut the sardines into slices the size of your middle finger. Arrange on a lightly greased baking tray.
2. Drizzle 2 tablespoons of olive oil over the fish and bake uncovered for about 5 minutes at 150°C/300°F, and drain.
3. Transfer the cooked sardines to a shallow glass or ceramic bowl.
4. Heat the rest of the olive oil in a frying pan. Sauté the onions and garlic until translucent. Blanch the tomatoes in boiling water for 30 seconds, plunge into ice water, remove and peel.
5. Stir in the tomatoes, white wine, rosemary, bay leaf, currants and sugar. Season with salt and black pepper.
6. Simmer uncovered for about 10 minutes or until the mixture thickens.
7. While the sauce is still hot, add vinegar and extra virgin olive oil.
8. Zest the lemon peel and add to the sauce.
9. Pour the sauce over the fish while they're still warm.
10. Allow to cool, cover and refrigerate overnight.
11. Remove bay leaf before serving.

Chef's note:

This dish can be served either as a meze (appetizer) or with a side of salad as a main course.

Ingredients: (serves 6)

- 1 kg fresh sardine filets
- ⅓ cup olive oil
- 1 medium red onion, finely diced
- 3 cloves garlic, crushed
- 200 g cherry tomatoes
- ½ cup white wine
- 1 tbsp fresh rosemary, chopped
- 1 bay leaf
- 2 tbsp currants
- ½ tsp sugar
- Salt, to taste
- Black Pepper, to taste
- ½ cup white wine vinegar or cider vinegar
- ½ cup extra virgin olive oil
- 1 lemon, peel of, grated

Grilled Grouper with Beet and Bulgur Salad

Aret Sahakyan

Preparation:

1. For the bulgur salad, place the beets in a pot with water to cover. Boil until tender and drain, reserving the cooking liquid.
2. Puree one of the beets in the reserved liquid with pomegranate syrup.
3. Put the bulgur in a small saucepan. Add the beet puree, season with salt and black pepper, and bring to a boil. Cover, remove from heat and put to one side.
4. Dice the remaining beets, place in a mixing bowl and combine with spring onions, mint, red wine vinegar, extra virgin olive oil and almonds and season with salt and black pepper. Use a fork to fluff the bulgur and mix the ingredients thoroughly.
5. Preheat the broiler or outdoor grill. Season the grouper filets with salt and black pepper. Then brush with olive oil and cook until slightly pink in the center.
6. To serve, arrange each serving of grilled fish on a bed of bulgur salad.

Ingredients: (serves 6)

- 6, 180 g grouper filets
- 2 tbsp extra virgin olive oil
- Salt, to taste
- Black Pepper, to taste

Ingredients for the Beet and Bulgur Salad:

- 4 medium beets
- 3 tbsp pomegranate syrup
- ½ cup fine bulgur, rinsed in cold water
- ¼ cup spring onions (scallions), chopped
- ¼ cup mint, chopped
- 2 tbsp red wine vinegar
- ¼ cup extra virgin olive oil
- ¼ cup slivered almonds
- Salt, to taste
- Black Pepper, to taste

Muhammara (Basted Grilled Prawns with Purslane and Yogurt Dressing)

Aret Sahakyan

Preparation:

1. To make the muhammara, roast the peppers directly over an open flame for 8-10 minutes, turning continuously so the skin chars evenly.

2. Place the charred peppers in a plate and cover with saran wrap so that it continues to steam and soften.

3. When the peppers are cooled, carefully peel away the blackened skin, and remove the stems, seeds and white membranes. Don't rinse, as this would wash away the smoky flavor.

4. Coarsely chop the peppers and transfer to a food processor along with all of the ingredients except for the extra virgin olive oil. Puree until coarse. Then, blend in the olive oil in a slow, steady stream until the mixture is creamy.

5. Remove the heads of the prawns. Use a paring knife to make an incision along the back of the prawns, leaving the shells intact. Remove the veins. Gently lift the shell and cover the flesh of each prawn with about 1 tablespoon of the muhammara paste.

6. Heat the broiler or outdoor grill and cook the prawns until pink, turning only once.

7. Just before serving, blend all of the ingredients for the yogurt sauce and toss with the purslane leaves.

8. Spoon equal portions of the purslane and yogurt sauce onto each plate, top with prawns and serve hot.

Ingredients: (serves 6)

- 18 fresh jumbo prawns or jumbo shrimp
- 2 cups purslane leaves, rinsed

Ingredients for the muhammara:

- 2 large red bell peppers
- 1 red hot chili pepper, remove seeds and chop
- 1 clove garlic, crushed with 1 tsp salt
- 75 g / ¾ cup coarsely chopped walnuts
- 10 g / ¼ cup fresh bread crumbs, lightly toasted
- 1 tbsp pomegranate syrup
- 1 lemon, juice of
- 1 tbsp hot water
- 60 ml / ¼ cup extra virgin olive oil

Ingredients for the yogurt sauce:

- ½ cup strained yogurt
- 2 tbsp fresh mint, finely chopped
- ½ lemon, juice of
- 3 tbsp extra virgin olive oil
- Salt, to taste
- Black Pepper, to taste

Broiled Red Mullet with Pine Nuts & Sumac Pesto

Aret Sahakyan

Preparation:

1. For the pine nut-sumac pesto sauce, combine the ingredients listed below.
2. Filet the fish and lightly season with salt and black pepper.
3. Arrange half of the fish filets, skin side down, on a baking tray. Coat each one with some of the sauce and place the remaining fish on top, skin side up, with the pesto sandwiched in between them. Bake at 180°C/350°F until cooked and slightly pink in the middle.
4. Arrange 3 filets on each plate, drizzle with olive oil, sprinkle with sumac and serve hot.

Chef's note:

Made from the ground drupes of the sumac bush, sumac powder is also used to give meat dishes a fruity-tart flavor.

Ingredients: (serves 6)

- 18 whole red mullets, 120 g each
- Salt, to taste
- Black Pepper, to taste
- Black Extra virgin olive oil

Pine Nut-Sumac Pesto:
- 3 tbsp pine nuts, toasted and chopped
- 2 tbsp fresh bread crumbs
- ¼ cup parsley, finely chopped
- 2 cloves garlic, grated
- 1 tbsp sumac
- 1 tsp lemon zest

Lakerda (Salted Bonito) and Fava

Deniz Alphan

Preparation of Lakerda:

1. Use only the middle section of the fish by cutting off the head at the level of the fins and the bottom of the fish five fingers above the tail. Thoroughly clean the middle section. Use a needle to remove any blood clots.
2. Cut the fish into 10 to 15 cm thick pieces. Soak in cold water for 6 hours, changing the water every hour. Rinse the fish thoroughly to remove all traces of blood. Place in a strainer to drain excess water and refrigerate for a few hours.
3. Sprinkle a generous amount of rock salt on the bottom of a wide container with a lid. Roll the fish in the salt and arrange in a row.
4. Sprinkle a generous amount of salt over the fish. Place a weight or plate over the top of the fish and cover with the lid, making certain the container is airtight. Place on the bottom shelf of the refrigerator.
5. The lakerda will be ready to eat after 10 days of refrigeration.
6. Before serving, rinse off the salt under running water and slice the lakerda with a sharp knife.
7. Serve with sliced red onions.

Preparation of Fava:

1. Sauté the finely diced onion on medium heat in a saucepan until translucent.
2. Place the fava beans in a pan, add onions and water to cover, bring to a boil and simmer. Add boiling water as the cooking water is absorbed.
3. Add sugar and season with salt and black pepper. Continue cooking until the beans are tender.
4. When the consistency reaches that of pudding, remove from heat and force through a strainer until smooth.
5. Add the chopped dill.
6. Spoon the fava into individual pre moistened serving cups.
7. Chill until firm.
8. Just before serving, remove fava from the cups into plates and drizzle with olive oil.

Ingredients: (serves 6)

Lakerda:

- Bonito, large or small
- Rock salt
- Red onion

Fava:

- 500 g dried fava beans
- 3 tbsp olive oil
- 1 bunch dill
- 1 ½ tsp sugar
- 1 large onion
- Salt and Black Pepper, to taste
- Lemon, juice of

Chef's note:

Lakerda *is normally made with mature bonito (torik) but the smaller bonito (palamut), can also be used. 1 whole torik or a large palamut makes enough lakerda to last all summer.*

Seared Scallops with Humus and Pastırma

Aret Sahakyan

Preparation:

1. Season scallops with salt and black pepper.
2. To make the humus, soak the beans overnight in cold water twice their volume. Drain the beans and rinse thoroughly the following day. Bring to a boil in a large pot of fresh water, lower the heat and simmer until tender.
3. Drain the beans. While still warm, puree in a food processor with the crushed garlic, cumin, lemon juice and olive oil.
4. Heat 2 tablespoons olive oil in a skillet and cook the pastırma until crisp. Remove and drain on a paper towel.
5. Wipe away the oil in the skillet and add 2 tablespoons fresh olive oil. When the oil is smoking hot, sear the seasoned scallops for 45 seconds on one side and 30 seconds on the other, without moving them. Drain on a paper towel.
6. To serve, spoon about 45 grams of humus onto each plate, place 3 strips of pastırma on the humus and arrange 3 scallops on top of the pastırma.

Chef's note:

Pastırma, also known as "bastourma", is a highly seasoned, air-dried beef. Can be substituted with bacon or prosciutto.

Ingredients: (serves 6)

- 60 ml / 4 tbsp olive oil
- 18 thin slices pastırma
- 18 jumbo scallops
- 270 g / ¾ cup humus
- Salt, to taste
- Black Pepper, to taste

Ingredients for White Bean Humus:

- 250 g / 1 cup dried white beans
- 1 clove garlic, crushed with 1 tsp salt
- ½ tsp cumin
- 1 lemon, juice of
- 3 tbsp olive oil
- Salt, to taste
- Black Pepper, to taste

Botargo on Phyllo Squares

Engin Akın

Preparation:

1. Preheat the oven to 180°C/350°F.
2. Grease a baking tray with butter.
3. Carefully place the sheet of phyllo on the baking tray.
4. Trim any overhanging phyllo pastry.
5. Using a sharp knife, cut the phyllo vertically and horizontally to create uniform squares of pastry.
6. Bake the phyllo pastry in the middle of the oven until golden brown and reserve for use later.
7. Serve by placing a lentil-size bit of butter on each phyllo square topped with a slice of botargo. Consume immediately.

Chef's note:

The phyllo will be more tasty if you take the time to heat both sides of the phyllo squares for a minute in a hot, non-stick cast iron skillet.

Botargo: This Mediterranean delicacy is the roe pouch of tuna, grey mullet or swordfish. It is massaged by hand to eliminate air pockets. It is then dried and cured in salt for a few weeks and then preserved in bees wax. Serve by peeling back the wax encasement and slicing.

Ingredients: (serves 6)

- 15-20 slices of botargo, no thicker than 2mm
- 1 sheet phyllo pastry
- 1 tbsp butter

Fish Soup with Wheat Berries

Marianna Yerasimos

Preparation:

1. In a bowl, soak the wheat berries overnight and then drain. The next day, soak saffron in ⅓ cup of vinegar for 2-3 hours.

2. In a heavy skillet, simmer the wheat berries in 4 cups of water for about 1-1 ½ hours, stirring occasionally, until the starch released from the wheat has settled in the pot. The time it takes for this to happen varies according to the type of wheat you're using. It's important, however, that you use wheat that will release starch. Drain the wheat, reserving the cooking liquid.

3. Set aside 400 grams of the cooking liquid and 100 grams of wheat.

4. Clean and rinse the fish and season with salt.

5. Roughly chop the onions, mint and parsley. Reserve 1-2 sprigs of parsley as garnish.

6. Heat butter in a large pot and sauté the onions.

7. When the onions are translucent, add the mint and the parsley and sauté for another 5 minutes.

8. Add 4 ¾ cups of water to the pot, along with ⅔ cup vinegar and a pinch of salt. Simmer on medium heat until the onions are soft.

9. Strain the wheat berry cooking liquid you reserved and empty into a different pot. Add the fish and cook for 15-20 minutes. Remove from heat and let cool.

10. Remove the fish from the pot. Remove the heads, skin and bones and set the remaining fish aside.

11. Bring the stock from the fish to a boil. Then slowly add the cooking liquid from the wheat and then the wheat berries. Bring to the boil and then simmer at low heat.

12. Whisk the egg yolks and lemon juice in a bowl. Stir in the wheat starch. Thin with 4-5 tablespoons of the broth. Add the saffron and vinegar, then slowly add the egg mixture to the soup, stirring continuously. When the soup begins to thicken, season with salt to taste and remove from the heat.

13. Place the reserved fish in a soup tureen and ladle the soup over them. Garnish with 1-2 sprigs of finely chopped parsley and serve.

Ingredients: (serves 6)

- 150 g / ⅔ cup wheat berries
- 1 lt / 4 cups water, for the wheat
- 1 kg fish (grey mullet or sea bass)
- 3 large onions
- 1 bunch parsley, finely chopped
- 1 bunch mint, finely chopped
- 6 tbsp butter
- 1 cup vinegar
- 2 tsp wheat starch
- 1.2 lt / 4 ¾ cups water
- 3 eggs yolks
- 1 lemon
- 0.5-1 g saffron
- Salt, to taste

Tarama (Cured Roe)

Deniz Alphan

Preparation:

1. Remove the membrane from the fish roe.
2. Soak the crustless bread briefly in water and squeeze out the excess water.
3. Combine the roe with the lemon juice and bread and slowly whisk in the olive oil, as though making mayonnaise. A hand whisk is best, but you may also use a hand held electric mixer, provided the fish eggs aren't crushed. Start very slowly, building up the speed gradually as you add the olive oil.
4. The mixture may seem a bit watery but it will absorb liquid while stored in the refrigerator. Cover with saran wrap so it doesn't dry out.

Ingredients: (serves 6)

- 150 g tarama (cured roe)
- 2-3 slices stale white bread, crusts removed
- 1 lemon, juice of
- 1 cup olive oil

Notes

Poultry

Aubergine Chicken Parcels

Vivet Rosales

Preparation:

1. Cut the aubergines lengthwise into 4 pieces. Fry the slices on both sides in ½ cup of olive until they are golden brown. Place them between sheets of paper towel to absorb the oil.

2. Heat 1 tablespoon of sunflower oil in a large saucepan and sauté the chopped onions until translucent. Stir in the diced banana peppers and sauté for an additional 3 minutes.

3. Cut the chicken into large chunks and add to the saucepan and sauté for another 5 minutes.

4. Add the peeled, chopped tomatoes and tomato paste.

5. Add thyme, salt, black pepper, bay leaf and l lt. boiling water. Simmer for about half an hour.

6. Remove the chicken pieces, leaving the liquid in the pan.

7. Arrange the strips of aubergine , crisscrossed on a clean counter. Place a spoonful of chicken in the middle of each and gather up the ends of the slices to form an envelope.

8. Place a tomato slice and a slice of bell pepper on top of each parcel and secure with a toothpick and arrange in a baking dish.

9. Add chicken boullon cubes to the stock used to boil the chicken and simmer on medium heat until reduced to a sauce-like consistency.

10. Pour the sauce over the aubergine pieces.

11. Bake in a preheated over for 20 minutes at 180°C/350°F.

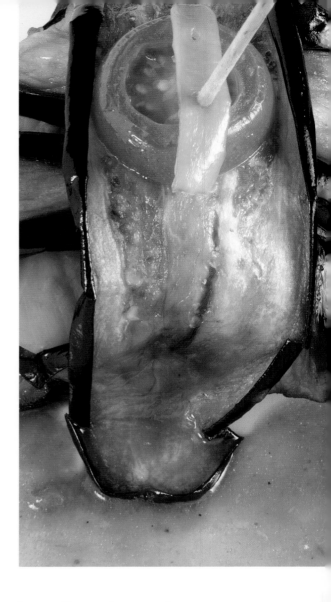

Ingredients: (serves 6)

- 1 kg boneless chicken (preferably thigh)
- 8 aubergines
- ½ cup olive oil
- 2 banana (yellow wax) peppers, diced
- 1 banana pepper and tomato, for garnish
- 1 yellow onion
- 1 bay leaf
- 5 tomatoes
- 1 tbsp tomato paste
- 2 sprigs fresh thyme
- 2 tsp salt
- 1 tsp black pepper
- 1 tbsp sunflower oil
- 2 chicken bouillon cubes

Turkey Stew with Zucchini Puree

Istanbul Culinary Institute

Preparation:

1. Heat olive oil in a saucepan and in turn, add onion, garlic, diced red bell pepper and banana peppers and sauté.
2. Add turkey and sauté for a few minutes. Add the shallots, tomato paste and chicken or vegetable stock (see page 79).
3. Season with half of the salt and black pepper and simmer for 25 minutes or until the turkey is thoroughly cooked.
4. Boil the zucchini until tender, drain and mash.
5. Melt butter in a large saucepan and add flour and sauté for 5-6 minutes. Add milk and whisk until it reaches a smooth consistency. Season with the remaining salt and black pepper. Turn off the heat and stir in the dill.
6. Plate the stewed turkey on a bed of pureed zucchini, pour the sauce over the top and serve hot.

Ingredients: (serves 6)

- 1.2 kg boneless turkey, cubed
- 4 ½ tsp olive oil
- 3 ½ tbsp butter
- 4-5 sprigs fresh thyme
- 2-3 cloves garlic, finely minced
- 1 large onion, finely chopped
- 6 large zucchini, rinsed and trimmed
- 2 ½ tbsp flour
- 2 ½ cups milk
- 10-15 shallots

- 6 banana (yellow wax) peppers, diced
- 1 large bell red pepper, diced
- 1 ½ tsp salt
- 1 ½ tsp black pepper
- 2 ¼ cup chicken or vegetable stock
- 1 ½ tbsp tomato paste
- ½ bunch dill, finely chopped

Duck Mutancana

Asitane Restaurant

Preparation:

1. Remove the skin of the duck and cube.
2. Melt butter in a large pot and add the duck. Sauté until the meat juices have mostly evaporated.
3. Add the onions and sauté for an additional 2-3 minutes.
4. Add flour and continue to sauté for another 1-2 minutes, then add warm water. Simmer for 40-45 minutes.
5. When the meat is about 10 minutes from being fully cooked, add grapes, honey, almonds and season with salt.
6. Just before serving, cut the dried figs and dried apricots into thin slices and sauté in butter for 1-2 minutes. Add the spices and herbs to sauce and pour over the duck and serve.

Chef's note:

The addition of seasonal red plums makes for a tasty twist on this Ottoman dish. Simply boil 12 plums until the peel splits and garnish each portion with two plums.

Ingredients: (serves 6)

- 900 g duck, cubed
- 250 g shallots
- ¾ cup almonds, blanched
- 1 ½ tbsp honey
- 2 tsp salt
- 3 ⅔ cups warm water
- ½ cup red grapes, washed and soaked in warm water for 15 minutes
- 12 dried apricots
- 1 ½ tbsp flour
- 2 tbsp butter

Ingredients for sauce:

- 12 dried figs
- 3 ½ tbsp butter
- 1 pinch sumac
- 1 pinch salt
- 1 pinch flat leaf parsley
- 1 pinch hot paprika

Aubergine Stuffed with Quail

Asitane Restaurant

Preparation:

1. Singe away any stray feathers, then clean and de-bone the quail.
2. Marinate quail for 1 hour in a mixture of olive oil, basil and salt.
3. Cut a lid in the aubergines and hollow out enough of the flesh to hold two quails per aubergine. Fry each aubergine in 2 tablespoons of olive oil, turning constantly so the skin is completely and evenly cooked. Place on paper towel to remove excess oil.
4. Fry the marinated quail in a non-stick frying pan until golden.
5. Add red pepper paste and flour and cook for another minute. Then add white wine and water and stir a couple of times.
6. Add honey, hot paprika and salt and cook for another 2-3 minutes until the sauce thickens.
7. Place two quails in each aubergine and arrange in a baking dish. Pour the sauce and bake in a preheated over for 15 minutes at 150°C/300°F.
8. Baste the stuffed aubergines occassionally with the sauce in the baking dish.
9. Place in a serving dish, arnish with parsley and serve.

Ingredients: (serves 6)

- 12 quail
- 6 medium globe aubergines
- 2 tbsp honey
- 1 cup white wine
- 1 tbsp red pepper paste
- ½ cup flour
- ½ tbsp sweet basil
- 1 ½ tsp hot paprika
- Salt, to taste
- 2 cups olive oil
- 2 lt water
- 8 sprigs flat leaf parsley, chopped

Pomegranate Quail Stuffed with Cinnamon Pilaf, Served with Pumpkin Potato Mash

Ümit Yüksel - Sheraton Istanbul Maslak Hotel

Preparation:

1. Slice open the quail breast and de-bone.
2. Rinse the rice and sauté in a small saucepan in 1 tbsp butter, sunflower oil and cinnamon. Add one cup boiling water and cook until the water is absorbed and leave to rest.
3. Season rice with salt and black pepper. Stuff each quail with the rice and secure with toothpicks. Bake in a preheated oven for 12-13 minutes at 180°C/350°F.
4. Cube and boil the pumpkin and potatoes. When tender, drain and mash them with 1tablespoon melted butter and milk. Season with salt and black pepper and mash.
5. To prepare the sauce, bake the bones and any other bits of the cleaned quail in the oven until they dry out. Place them in a pot with the diced onion, carrot, garlic and tomato paste. Sauté until all of the ingredients are golden.
6. Then add just enough red wine to cover the mixture and then add water. Simmer for 1 hour and then strain the stock into a bowl.
7. Add pomegranate juice to stock and season with salt and black pepper.
8. Place the quail on a serving dish and sprinkle with pomegranate seeds. Drizzle the sauce over the top and garnish with fresh thyme. Serve hot with the pumpkin potato mash.

Ingredients: (serves 6)

- 6 whole quail
- Salt, to taste
- Black pepper, to taste
- 150 g / ¾ cup rice
- 2 tbsp butter
- 1 tbsp sunflower oil
- 3 potatoes, peeled
- ½ cup milk
- 1 chunk pumpkin, size of 1 potato
- ½ pomegranate, seeds only
- 2 tsp cinnamon

For the sauce:

- 1 yellow onion
- ½ carrot
- 1 clove garlic
- 1 tbsp tomato paste
- 1 cup red wine
- ½ cup pomegranate juice
- Salt and Black Pepper, to taste
- Water
- 3 sprigs fresh thyme, for garnish

Şıps (Chicken with Spiced Sauce)

Zeynep Çelikkan Kakınç

Preparation:

1. Wash and pat dry drumsticks, without removing skins. Place in a pot and cover with water and add a pinch of salt. Peel and halve an onion. Peel the garlic bulb, cutting each clove in half. Add to the pot and bring to the boil.

2. When the drumsticks are cooked remove the skins and place on a separate plate. Pour the stock through a strainer and blend the remains in a food processor or blender.

3. For the sauce, chop the remaining onion. Heat butter in a large saucepan and sauté until onions are translucent. Season with hot paprika and salt and add a bit of the stock. Finally, add the vegetable mixture from the blender and coriander powder.

4. Stir the flour into the milk, add to the sauce and continue simmering.

5. When the sauce is cooked, add fresh coriander and drumsticks and stir until the chicken is thoroughly coated with the sauce. Remove from the heat.

6. Let the chicken stand for 30 minutes before serving.

Ingredients: (serves 6)

- 12 chicken drumsticks, with skins
- 1 large bulb garlic
- 6 tbsp butter
- 2 yellow onions
- 1 ½ tbsp hot paprika
- 1 tbsp coriander
- 2 ⅓ cup milk
- 7 tbsp all purpose or corn flour
- 5 sprigs fresh coriander, chopped

Çılbır (Poached Eggs with Yogurt Sauce)

Istanbul Culinary Institute

Preparation:

1. Add vinegar and salt to a heavy saucepan of water deep enough so that the eggs won't sink to the bottom. Bring to a boil and reduce to simmer.
2. Break each egg into a small bowl and then gently scoop an egg into the boiling water and stir the water to create a vortex. Use a spoon to nudge the white closer to the yolk. You can cook up to four eggs at a time, undisturbed, for 3-5 minutes depending on how firm you want the yolk, which should be slightly runny.
3. Use a slotted spoon to remove the eggs to a pre-heated plate.
4. Crush garlic with a mortar and pestle or with the side of a knife on a cutting board and whisk into the yogurt until smooth.
5. Heat butter in a small saucepan and add hot paprika.
6. Spoon the yogurt sauce over the eggs, then drizzle hot butter and serve immediately.

Ingredients: (serves 6)

- 12 eggs, room temperature
- 6 cups water
- ¾ tbsp salt
- 2 tbsp white vinegar
- 3 cups yogurt, room temperature
- 3 cloves garlic
- 2 tbsp butter
- 1 ½ tbsp hot paprika

Menemen (Scrambled Eggs with Tomatoes and Banana Peppers)

Istanbul Culinary Institute

Preparation:

1. Heat olive oil in a non-stick medium sized saucepan.
2. Sauté the banana peppers and then add the tomatoes. Season with salt and black pepper.
3. When most of the liquid has reduced, stir in the cheese and parsley.
4. Break the eggs directly into the saucepan and stir.
5. Once the eggs have cooked, serve hot.

Ingredients: (serves 6)

- 12 eggs
- 2 ½ tbsp olive oil
- 3 medium tomatoes, cubed
- 8 banana (yellow wax) peppers, medium cubes
- 2 thick slices of firm white (feta) cheese, grated
- Salt, to taste
- Black Pepper, to taste
- ½ bunch parsley, finely chopped

Meat

Lamb Entrecote with Pomegranate Glaze and Apricot

Mehmet Gürs

Preparation:

Preparation of Lamb Marinade:

1. Peel the garlic cloves.
2. Remove the stems of the rosemary sprigs.
3. Mix rosemary leaves and garlic with the olive oil in a blender until very smooth. Otherwise, the marinade will burn during cooking.
4. Marinade the lamb overnight.

Preparation of Honey & Herb Apricot Confit:

1. Cut the apricots in half crosswise. Remove the stems from the herbs.
2. Combine all of the ingredients, arrange on a tray and bake for 30 minutes at 100°C/210°F.
3. If the apricots dry out while cooking add a bit of honey and olive oil.
4. Allow to cool on the tray and then remove the rosemary and thyme leaves.
5. Store apricots, covered, at room temperature.

Preparation of Pomegranate glaze:

1. Reduce the juice to one-fourth its size.
2. In a separate saucepan, heat the oil with garlic and chilli.
3. Add the remaining ingredients and the pomegranate reduction. Bring to a boil and then simmer for 2 minutes.
4. Strain, cover and let the glaze rest at room temperature.

Ingredients: (serves 6)

Ingredients for the Lamb Marinade:

- Six 170 g rack of lamb, de-boned and trimmed of fat, 12 portions
- 1 ¼ cup virgin olive oil
- 5 sprigs fresh rosemary, leaves only
- 8-10 cloves garlic

Ingredients for Honey & Herb Apricot Confit:

- ⅔ cup / 18 natural, sun-dried apricots
- ½ cup honey
- ⅓ cup virgin olive oil
- 1 sprig fresh thyme, leaves only
- 1 sprig fresh rosemary, leaves only

Ingredients for Pomegranate Glaze:

- ½ cup fresh pomegranate juice
- ½ tbsp 'Urfa' chilli pepper
- 3 cloves garlic, mashed to a paste
- 4 tbsp virgin olive oil
- ⅓ cup honey

Confit

Preparation:

1. Remove the lamb from the marinade and wipe off excess liquid.
2. Quickly sear on both sides in a dry saucepan and then transfer to a baking tray. Brush pomegranate glaze on each piece.
3. Bake at 250°C/480°F until rare. (Internal meat temperature should be 60°C/140°F after resting for 3 minutes.)
4. Take lamb out of the oven and brush with the glaze again.
5. Set aside covered for 2 minutes. (Internal meat temperature should be about 60°C/140°F after resting.)
6. Brush the serving dishes diagonally with the glaze.
7. Slice the lamb into strips 2-cm thick and arrange 3 strips on each plate on top of the glaze.
8. Garnish each plate with 3 apricot halves on the side.

Chef's note:

Lamb "entrecote" is rack of lamb that has been de-boned and trimmed of fat. This recipe calls for the Kıvırcık breed of lamb from Thrace, which is flavorful, tender and pale pink. Urfa Chilli is moderately hot, crushed red peppers known as "Urfa Biberi".

Ali Nazik Kebab

Mabeyin Restaurant

Preparation:

1. Prick the skins of the aubergines and roast over hot coals or in the oven . (See page 79)
2. After cooling, peel skins and chop into small pieces.
3. Brown the meat of your choice. Once the meat juices are released and cooked off, add butter and season with salt.
4. Turn off heat and season with hot paprika and black pepper.
5. Whisk the yogurt and crushed garlic in a bowl until it reaches a creamy consistency.
6. Add the aubergines into the garlic yogurt and pour into a serving dish.
7. Arrange the meat over the yogurt sauce and serve.

Chef's note:

You can substitute the leg of lamb with chuck steak.

Ingredients: (serves 6)

- 1 kg globe aubergines
- 250 g leg of lamb, cut into small pieces
- 250 g / 1 ¼ cup strained yogurt, room temperature
- 3-4 cloves garlic, grated
- Salt, to taste
- Black Pepper, to taste
- Hot paprika, to taste
- 2 tbsp butter

Lamb Ragoût with Prunes

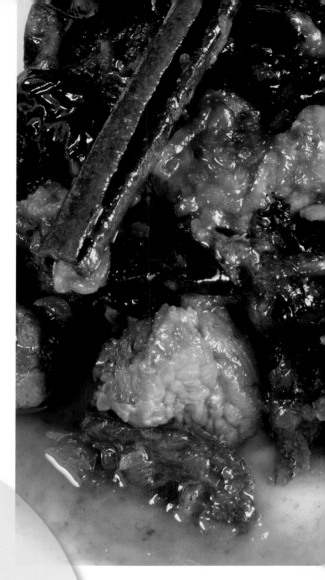

Dr. Özge Samancı

Preparation:

1. Place the lamb in a pot, cover with water, bring to the boil and cook until tender.
2. Skim the foam off the top, cook for a few more minutes and remove from heat.
3. Remove the meat with a slotted spoon and place in a bowl, reserving the stock in the pot for later use.
4. Strain the juice from the three grated onions, reserving the onions for step 7.
5. Marinate lamb in the onion juice for ten minutes.
6. Heat butter in a large and shallow saucepan, brown the lamb and remove to a bowl.
7. Brown the onions in the pan drippings.
8. Add the prunes and sauté and stir for a couple of minutes.
9. Add the lamb, reserved stock, cinnamon sticks, sugar and salt.
10. Simmer on low heat for about 1 hour or until the meat is tender. Serve hot.

Chef's note:

Chestnuts, dried apricots or quince can be substituted for the prunes.

Ingredients: (serves 6)

- 900 g boneless lamb shoulder, cut into 2 cm cubes
- 3 medium onions, roughly grated
- 6 tbsp butter
- 300 g pitted black prunes
- 2 tbsp sugar
- 3 cinnamon sticks
- 1 ½ tsp salt

Baked Lamb Chop Börek

Gönül Paksoy

Preparation:

1. Peel the onion and roughly grate.
2. Combine the salt, black pepper, crushed pink peppercorns, crushed cumin, thyme and onion. Spread 1 tsp of this mixture over each of the lamb chops. Pile them in a covered dish and marinate in the refrigerator overnight.
3. Cut the phyllo pastry into 8-cm wide long strips.
4. Combine the olive oil, yogurt, cream and egg and lightly brush this mixture on one side of the phyllo. Wrap a triangle of phyllo and fold up like a flag around the meat of each lamb chop, leaving the rib uncovered.
5. Arrange them on a greased baking tray, brush with olive oil and sprinkle with poppy seeds, if desired.
6. Bake for 30 minutes at 200°C/390°C and serve hot.

Chef's note:

Once you've completed step 5 of this recipe, you can freeze the lamb chops and bake later.

Ingredients: (serves 6)

- 12 small lamb chops
- 1 onion
- 1 tbsp black pepper
- 2 tsp pink peppercorns, crushed
- 2 tsp coriander seeds, crushed
- 1 tsp thyme
- 2 sheets of phyllo pastry
- ¼ cup olive oil
- ¼ cup yogurt
- 2 tbsp cream
- 1 egg
- Poppy seeds, to taste
- Salt, to taste

Abugannuş (Lamb Cubes on a Bed of Grilled Vegetables)

Mabeyin Restaurant

Preparation:

1. Prick the skin of the aubergines, banana peppers and tomatoes with a fork. Roast in the broiler, turning occasionally, until the skins blacken.
2. Remove skins and chop into small pieces.
3. In a saucepan, melt 1 tbsp of butter and sauté the lamb until cooked.
4. In a non-stick saucepan, heat and mix the roasted aubergines, tomatoes and banana peppers.
5. Season vegetables with salt, black pepper and hot paprika.
6. Serve the lamb on a bed of grilled vegetables.
7. Drizzle with melted butter , garnish with parsley and serve hot.

Ingredients: (serves 6)

- 1 kg aubergines
- 700 g tomatoes
- 200 g banana (yellow wax) peppers
- 1 kg boneless leg of lamb, cubed
- 100 g / 6 tbsp butter
- Salt, to taste
- Black Pepper, to taste
- Hot paprika, to taste
- Parsley, for garnish

Şans Kebab

Şans Restaurant

Preparation:

1. In a saucepan, heat butter and sauté onions and garlic and cool.
2. In a large bowl, knead ground veal and lamb, black pepper, cumin, hot paprika flakes and add to the onions and garlic and mix well.
3. Marinate lamb breast filets in olive oil, thyme and salt.
4. Preheat the broiler or barbeque grill.
5. With the ground meat mixture, prepare oval sized meatballs and line on a skewer and grill.
6. Grill lamb breast filets. When cooked, cut into long strips.
7. Grill tomato wedges and banana peppers
8. Cut pita bread into cubes and fry in a tablespoon of melted butter in a saucepan until they are crispy
9. Arrange pita bread on a serving dish and pour yogurt over the bread. Place the strips of lamb breast filets and meatballs over the yogurt.
10. Garnish with grilled tomatoes and banana peppers.
11. Drizzle melted butter, sprinkle with hot paprika and serve hot.

Ingredients: (serves 6)

- 300 g ground veal (chuck)
- 300 g ground lamb breast
- 300 g lamb breast filets
- 1 clove garlic, finely chopped
- 1 onion, finely chopped
- 2 cups yogurt, room temperature
- 6 tbsp butter
- 1 tsp hot paprika
- 1 tsp cumin
- 1 tsp black pepper
- Salt, to taste
- 2 large tomatoes, quartered
- 6 banana (yellow wax) peppers
- Flat bread or pita bread, enough for 6 servings

For the marinade:

- 4 tbsp olive oil
- 1 tsp thyme
- Salt, to taste

Beetroot Ayran (Yogurt Drink) & Ground Meat Breadsticks

Eyüp Kemal Sevinç - Founder, Hobimle Mutluyum Culinary Arts School

Preparation:

1. To peel the tomato, carve out the stem and cut an "x" in the bottom of the tomato. Bring a saucepan of water to a boil and prepare an ice bath in a bowl. Place the tomato in the boiling water for 30 seconds then immediately plunge it into the ice water. The peel will now slip off easily. Then remove the seeds and quarter.

2. Mix the ground veal, tomato, hot green peppers, garlic, onion, parsley, salt and black pepper in a food processor or blender to prepare the filling.

3. Combine the flour, water and yeast and let rest.

4. When the yeast has been activated, roll the dough out on a well-floured surface into circles 30-35 cm in diameter, ensuring they don't stick to the countertop or rolling pin.

5. When the dough is sufficiently thin, place the filling in a thin line in the center of each, roll up to about the size and shape of a breadstick and cut. Repeat and continue until the dough and filling is finished.

6. Brush breadsticks with egg batter and bake for 12 minutes at 180°C/350°F.

7. In a separate bowl, prepare the yogurt drink by whisking the strained yogurt, mineral water and season with salt to taste.

8. Puree the pickled beets in a food processor.

9. Whisk the puree into the yogurt drink until it reaches the desired color and consistency.

10. Serve in shot glasses.

11. Cut the breadsticks diagonally and place on top of each shot glass.

Chef's note:

Popular in the Balkans and parts of Asia, ayran is a refreshing beverage prepared with yogurt, water (or mineral water) and a dash of salt. In some regions, milk is used instead of water. The most flavorful ayran is made with sheep's milk yogurt.

Ingredients: (serves 6)

- 60 g / ¼ cup strained yogurt
- 20 g / 2 tbsp pickled beets
- 50 ml / ¼ cup mineral water
- 100 g ground veal breast
- 20 g yellow onion
- 10 g parsley
- 5 g garlic
- 50 g / 1 medium tomato, peeled
- 15 g / 2-3 hot green peppers
- 200 g / 1 ⅔ cups flour
- 50 ml / 3 tbsp water
- 10 g yeast
- 1 tsp salt
- 1 tsp black pepper
- Egg, to brush on the bread

Shoulder of Lamb with Hünkârbeğendi (Sultan's Delight)

Borsa Restaurant

Preparation:

1. Rub the lamb shoulders with citric acid and suet (or olive oil and butter) and broil both sides in the oven at 300°C/575°F.
2. When lamb has browned, cover with aluminon foil and bake for an hour and a half.

Preparation of the Hünkârbeğendi (Sultan's Delight):

1. Roast the aubergines in a hot oven or over an open flame for 8-10 minutes, turning them occasionally. While still hot, grip the stem and strip away the charred skin with a knife. Remove the clusters of large seeds.
2. Melt half of the butter in sauce pan.
3. Add the aubergines and mash them with a wooden spoon.
4. In a separate saucepan, melt the remaining butter on medium heat. Add flour and sauté for 6-8 minutes. Gradually add milk, stirring constantly to prevent lumps.
5. Add the aubergines and cook on medium heat for 5-6 minutes.
6. Add the grated cheese and stir.
7. Season with salt and keep warm until time to serve.

Preparation of the Pilaf:

1. Place the rice in a bowl, fill with warm water to cover and add 1 tbsp salt.
2. After the rice has soaked for an hour, rinse it in plenty of cold water and strain.
3. Soak the currants in a separate bowl of warm water until plump.
4. Melt butter in a pot, add and sauté pine nuts until golden brown. Add the chopped onions and sauté for an additional 4-5 minutes.
5. Add rice and continue cooking for an additional 8-10 minutes. Stir in the currants, allspice, cinnamon, cumin and black pepper.
6. Add the hot beef stock. Season withh salt, stir with a wooden spoon and cover with a lid.
7. Bring to a boil, lower to simmer and cook for 15 minutes or until the liquid is totally absorbed.
8. When the rice is fully cooked, remove from heat.
9. Remove lid, place a gauze or cotton cloth over the pot and put the lid back on.
10. Let the pilaf stand for 10-15 minutes, then gently stir with a wooden spoon.

& Pilaf

Ingredients: (serves 6)

For the Lamb Tandır:

- 6, 400 g shoulder of lamb, on the bone
- 1 tbsp rock salt
- 1 ½ tsp citric acid
- 500 lamb suet or 250 g butter + 250 ml olive oil

For the Hünkârbeğendi:

- 2 kg globe aubergines
- 1 cup fresh kaşar or provolone cheese, grated
- 1 cup milk, warm
- 1 tsp salt
- 1 ½ tbsp flour
- 5 tbsp butter

For the Pilaf:

- 1 ⅓ cups rice
- 1 yellow onion, finely chopped
- 2 tbsp pine nuts
- 2 tbsp currants
- 1 tsp allspice
- ½ tsp black pepper
- ½ tsp cumin
- ¼ tsp cinnamon
- 2 ½ tbsp butter
- 2 cups beef stock, hot

Grilled Loin of Lamb with Smoked Aubergine Puree, Chard and Mustard Grain Sauce

Sunset Grill & Bar

Preparation:

Preparation of Aubergine Puree:

1. Roast the red bell peppers over an open flame or hot oven, turning occasionally. When they've cooled, cut off the tops.

2. Prick aubergines in a few places with a fork. Roast over an open flame or hot oven, turning occasionally until the skins are charred and aubergine tender, about 20-25 minutes, depending on size.

3. While still hot, grip the stem and use a knife to strip away the charred skin. Then cut off the stems and remove large seeds from the cavity.

4. Melt butter in a saucepan and add flour. Sauté the flour on low heat until it begins to turn golden brown. Slowly add warm milk stirring constantly to prevent lumps. Stir in the cheese.

5. Season with salt and black pepper and stir until the mixture is smooth. When it begins bubbling remove it from heat.

6. When the red peppers have cooled, stuff them with equal portions of the aubergine puree.

Preparation of Stuffed Swiss Chard:

1. In a saucepan, sauté the wild mushrooms and goat cheese in butter. Season with salt and black pepper

2. Plunge the Swiss chard leaves into hot water. Remove and uising the handle of a knife, crush the veins. Divide each leaf into 2 or 3 pieces, depending on size.

3. Place 1-1½ teaspoons of the sautéed mushroom mixture on a piece of leaf and roll up as you would a grape leaf.

Preparation of main dish:

1. Grill the lamb on barbeque or broil.

2. While the lamb is grilling, bring the mustard sauce ingredients to a boil.

3. Pour the mustard sauce on a serving dish and place stuffed Swiss chard on plate.

4. Place the grilled lamb on top of the stuffed Swiss chard.

5. Arrange the stuffed peppers on the plate around the lamb.

6. Garnish with fresh sprigs of thyme and serve.

Stuffed Red Peppers, Stuffed Swiss

Ingredients: (serves 6)

- 1 ½ kg, 6 loin of lamb, boneless
- 120 g Aubergine Puree
- Stuffed Swiss Chard

For Aubergine Puree:

- 1 cup flour
- 6 globe aubergines
- 6 grilled red bell peppers
- 4 ¾ cups milk, warm
- 8 tbsp butter
- 3 cups kaşar or provolone cheese, grated
- Salt, to taste
- Black Pepper, to taste

For the Stuffed Swiss Chard:

- 120 wild mushrooms
- ⅔ cup goat cheese
- 12 leaves of Swiss chard
- 8 tbsp butter
- Salt, to taste
- Black Pepper, to taste

For the Mustard Sauce:

- 2 tbsp grain mustard
- 2 tbsp butter
- 1 cup beef stock

Cherry Wood Smoked Loin of Lamb with White Bean

Mehmet Gürs

Preparation:

Preparation of Loin of Lamb:

1. Brush the lamb with olive oil. Sprinkle with salt and sugar and leave to marinate while preparing the smoker.
2. Fill a stovetop smoker with sawdust, cover and place over medium heat. The moment the sawdust starts smoking, open cover, quickly place the lamb in the smoker and tightly close the cover.
3. Smoke over medium high heat for 2-3 minutes, depending on the thickness of the lamb. Remove from the cooker.
4. Sear quickly in a hot, dry saucepan.
5. Use immediately or refrigerate covered until service.

Preparation of White Bean Puree:

Day 1:

1. Place all ingredients in a pot and simmer on low heat until beans are tender.
2. Place in a small container, cool, then cover and refrigerate overnight.

Day 2:

3. Take the beans out of the refrigerator, transfer to a pot and heat thoroughly, adding water if necessary.
4. When the beans are heated, remove the bay leaves and thyme.
5. Puree the beans in a food processor fitted with a steel blade until smooth.
6. Pass through a fine mesh sieve.
7. Cover and keep warm until service

Ingredients: (serves 6)

Ingredients for Loin of Lamb:

- 6, 170 g "Trakya Kıvırcık" loin of lamb loins, boneless and trimmed of fat
- 3 tbsp extra virgin olive oil
- 1 pinch sea salt
- 1 pinch sugar
- Cherry wood sawdust, as needed

Ingredients for White Bean Puree:

- 300 g dried white beans, soaked overnight, rinsed and drained
- 1 lt chicken stock
- 1 2/3 cups water
- 1 cup extra virgin olive oil
- 4 cloves garlic
- 3 fresh bay leaves
- 4 large sprigs thyme
- 5 white peppercorns
- 1 pinch fine sea salt

Puree and Walnut Pâté

Preparation of the Walnut Paté:

1. Pulse all ingredients except olive oil in a blender.
2. Slowly add olive oil, and puree until smooth.
3. Put paté inside a squeeze bottle to mould on the serving plates.
4. Set aside and keep cool.

Just before serving:

1. Heat the loin of lamb for 3 minutes in the oven at 250°C/250°C. Remove.
2. Allow to rest, covered, for 5 minutes. After resting, the inner temperature of the meat should be about 60°C/140°F.
3. Slice each loin diagonally and serve with the bean puree and walnut paté.

Ingredients for Walnut Paté:

- 1 cup walnuts
- 1 cup aged kaşar or provolone cheese, grated
- 4 cloves garlic
- 1 pinch fine sea salt
- 1 pinch cracked black pepper
- 1 ½ cups virgin olive oil

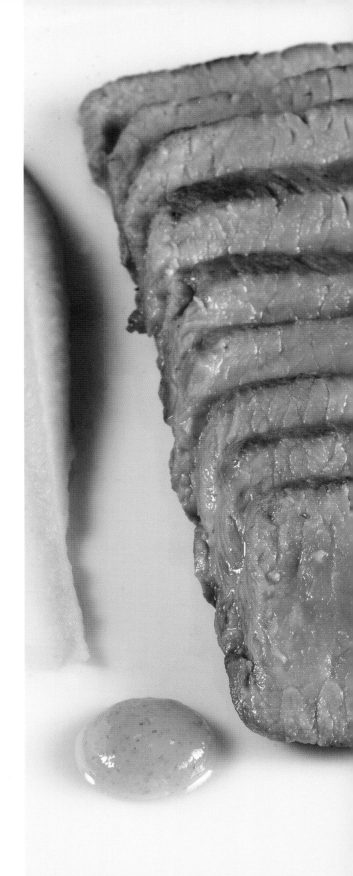

Marinated Lamb Chops with Smoked Aubergine Risotto

Maximillian J.W. Thomae - Executive Chef, Pera Palas Hotel

Preparation:

Preparation of the lamb:

1. Combine milk, fenugreek, olive oil and salt.
2. Marinate the lamb chops in this mixture for up to 3 days, and grill on barbeque or broil.

Preparation of thyme sauce:

1. Bake the bones of the lamb in oven at 175°C/350°F for 40-45 minutes.
2. Peel and dice all of the vegetables except the potato. In a large pot, heat 1½ tablespoons sunflower oil, add garlic and vegetables and sauté . Add tomato paste and continue to sauté.
3. Add the bones and red wine, and bring to a boil.
4. Add water and simmer on low heat for 8 hours.
5. Strain to remove the bones and vegetables.
6. Add thyme and grated raw potato to thicken the sauce.

Ingredients: (serves 6)

Ingredients for Marinated Lamb:

- 24, lamb chops (40g)
- 75 ml / ⅓ cup milk
- 30 g fenugreek seeds, ground
- 150 ml / ⅔ cup olive oil
- Salt, to taste

Ingredients for Thyme Sauce:

- 1 kg bones of a lamb
- 1 celeriac
- 1 carrot
- 1 yellow onion
- 1 bulb garlic
- 2 lt / 8 cups water
- 1 ½ tbsp sunflower oil
- 75 cl / 3 cups red wine
- 50 g / 1 tbsp tomato paste
- 1 potato, grated
- 1 tsp wild thyme

Preparation of the Risotto:

1. Chop onion and garlic. In saucepan, heat olive oil and add ingredients and sauté.

2. Add rice and continue to sauté.

3. Add diced, grilled aubergine. (See page 79))

4. Pour in the white wine and stir until the rice has absorbed the wine.

5. Gradually add a little chicken stock, continuously stirring. Add more chicken stock when the liquid is absorbed. Repeat this step until the rice is fully cooked.

6. Then, stir in the parmesan cheese, butter and diced tomatoes.

7. When texture of the risotto is creamy, season with salt and black pepper and remove from the heat.

Ingredients for Risotto:

- 150 g / ¾ cup carnaroli rice
- 1 yellow onion
- 3 cloves garlic
- 1 ½ globe aubergines
- 1 ½ tomatoes
- 15 cl / ²/₃ cup white wine (sauvignon blanc)
- 450 ml / 1 ¾ cups chicken stock
- 75 g / ¾ cup parmesan cheese
- 60 g / 4 tbsp butter
- 30 ml / 3 tbsp olive oil
- Salt, to taste
- Black Pepper, to taste

Veal Cheeks with Tomato Pesto and Orzo

Ümit Yüksel - Sheraton Istanbul Maslak Hotel

Preparation:

1. Place veal cheeks, onion, carrot, thyme and sunflower oil in a small baking dish and cook in a preheated oven for 2 hours at 180°C/350°C.

2. In a deep saucepan, add butter, sunflower oil and orzo and sauté for a few minutes. When the orzo begins to change color, add 1 diced tomato and the diced banana pepper. Add water and simmer on low heat for 15-20 minutes. Remove from heat, cover and leave to rest. Then, gently stir in finely chopped mint.

3. Sauté the garlic in a small non-stick frying pan without oil. Add the remaining tomatoes and continue to sauté until cooked. Then puree with a hand blender.

4. Drain oil from the veal cheeks. Spoon the tomato pesto over the veal and serve hot with the orzo pilaf.

Ingredients: (serves 6)

- 1 ¹⁄₃ kg veal cheeks, cleaned
- 4 sprigs fresh thyme
- 2 ¾ cups sunflower oil
- 1 tbsp sunflower oil, for the orzo
- 1 carrot, julienned
- 1 onion, julienned
- ¾ cup orzo
- 4 small tomatoes, diced
- 1 green banana pepper, diced
- 1 tbsp butter
- 1 clove garlic, finely chopped
- ¼ bunch fresh mint, finely chopped
- 1 ½ cups water

Veal or Lamb Shish Kebab

Beyti Restaurant

Preparation:

1. Mix olive oil, wine and onion juice for the marinade.
2. Cut the meat into cubes 5 cm x 2 cm and marinade for up to 24 hours (minimum 2 hours).
3. Skewer the meat and grill, preferably over a charcoal or wood fire.
4. Adjust grilling time according to taste.

Chef's note:

For best results, use the boneless medallions of veal cut from the leg of the tenderloin. You can also use tenderloin of beef to prepare this recipe.

Ingredients: (serves 6)

- 1 kg boneless veal or lamb tenderloins
- 1 tbsp olive oil
- ½ tbsp red wine
- ¼ onion, juice of
- Salt

Kadınbudu Köfte (Lady's Thigh Meat Patties)

Istanbul Culinary Institute

Preparation:

1. Wash rice and drain. Bring water to a boil, add the rice and cook for 5-10 minutes. Drain excess water and let the rice cool.

2. Brown half of the ground lamb and veal in a saucepan with some olive oil.

3. Add onions and continue to sauté. Remove from heat and, when cool, place in a large bowl. Mix in the remaining uncooked ground meat.

4. Then add 1 egg, rice, salt and black pepper and knead thoroughly for 10 minutes. To prepare, take a piece of the mixture and make a ball roughly the size of an egg. Then, flatten it slightly in the palm of our hand to create an oval shape. Repeat until the mixture is used up.

5. Use enough sunflower oil to fill a pan about halfway, or 4-cm deep. Beat 5 eggs in a bowl with a fork. Roll the köfte in flour, dip into the bowl of eggs and deep fry, cooking evenly on all sides.

6. Spread a paper towel on a platter and transfer the köfte when done. Serve warm.

Chef's note:

Not all meat patties are grilled. This dish was called "Lady's Thigh Köfte" because the meat patties resemble the rounded thighs of a voluptuous woman. This dish was a favorite of the Ottoman court.

Ingredients: (serves 6)

- 240 g ground lamb
- 360 g ground veal
- 2 onions, finely chopped
- ½ cup rice
- ½ cup water
- 6 eggs
- Sunflower oil, for deep frying
- Flour, to coat the köfte
- Salt, to taste
- Black Pepper, to taste

Mini Meatballs in Lemon Sauce

Lâle Apa

Preparation:

1. Wash and drain rice. Combine with ground beef, onion, parsley, basil, salt and black pepper. Knead until well mixed.
2. Spread a couple of tablespoons of flour on a tray and fill a small bowl with water. Shape the meat mixture into bite size meatballs. (Dip your hands into the water to keep the mixture from sticking.)
3. Place the meatballs on the tray and shake back and forth until the meatballs are lightly coated with flour.
4. Wash the carrots, celery stalks and potatoes and dice.
5. Bring 4-5 cups water and butter to the boil in a pot. Add the carrots and celery. While they're not quite tender, add the meatballs and potatoes and season with salt. Simmer gently.
6. Add about a teaspoon of the flour left on the tray. Stir occasionally to prevent the meatballs from sticking to the bottom of the pot. Remove from heat when cooked. Reheat just before you add the sauce.

For the sauce:

1. Just before serving the meatballs, whisk 1 or 2 eggs (depending on how thick you want your sauce) in a small bowl with fresh lemon juice (1-2 tablespoons depending on how tart you want your sauce). Slowly add about half a cup of the cooking liquid from the pot of meatballs, stirring constantly so the mixture doesn't curdle.
2. Pour the lemon egg sauce into the pot with the meatballs. Serve hot immediately.

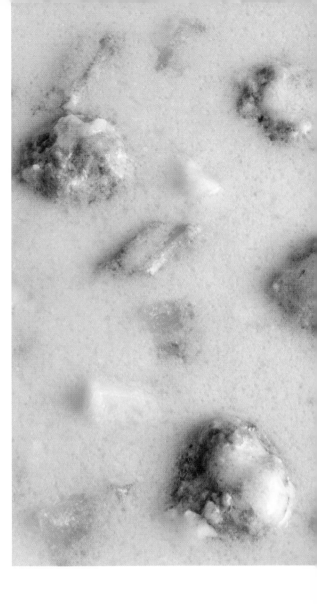

Ingredients: (serves 6)

- 500 g ground beef
- 1 bunch flat leaf parsley, chopped
- 4 basil leaves, chopped
- 1 large onion, roughly grated
- 2 heaping tbsp rice
- 1-2 tbsp flour
- 2-3 carrots, diced
- 2-3 celery stalks, diced, stringy part removed
- 2-3 potatoes, diced
- ½ cup butter
- Salt, to taste
- Black and pink peppercorns, fresh ground, to taste

For the sauce:

- 1-2 eggs
- Lemon juice, as needed

Bulgur Köfte (Meatballs) with Yogurt & Crispy Potatoes

Istanbul Culinary Institute

Preparation:

1. Soak chickpeas for a minimum of 8 hours and drain.
2. Boil chickpeas in a pot of water until tender.
3. Soak the fine bulgur in warm water for 15-20 minutes.
4. Preheat the oven to 160°C/320°F.
5. Prepare the meatball mixture by combining the ground veal, bulghur, two-thirds of the chopped onions, egg, mint, thyme, mint, parsley, allspice, cumin, black pepper, bread crumbs and salt. Knead until well mixed.
6. Shape the meatball mixture into walnut sized balls and arrange on a greased baking sheet. Place in preheated oven for about 10 minutes or until golden.
7. Heat 2 tablespoons sunflower oil in a large ovenproof pot and sauté the remaining onions, garlic and tomato paste. Add the tomatoes and chickpeas. Add just enough vegetable stock (see page 79) to cover. Bring to a boil and immediately reduce to a simmer.
8. Add the meatballs and simmer for 15 minutes. Then place the pot in the bottom shelf of the oven.
9. Peel the potato and slice into thin matchsticks. Deep-fry until golden brown and drain on a paper towel.
10. Place the matchstick potatoes in the middle of a serving dish. Spoon the chickpeas, sauce and meatballs over the potatoes and pour the whipped yogurt on top.

Ingredients: (serves 6)

- 600 g ground veal
- 1 cup chickpeas, dried
- ¾ cup fine bulgur
- 2 medium onions, finely chopped
- 1 clove garlic, finely chopped
- 2 medium tomatoes, peeled and diced
- 1 egg
- 1 ½ tbsp dried mint
- 1 ½ tbsp dried thyme
- ½ bunch flat lead parsley, finely chopped
- 1 tbsp allspice
- 1 tbsp cumin
- 1 tbsp black pepper
- 2 tbsp salt
- 3 tbsp bread crumbs
- 1 large potato
- 1 ½ tbsp tomato paste
- 1 ¾ cup sunflower oil
- 1 ½ cups yogurt, whipped at room temperature
- Vegetable stock, as needed

Basil Köfte (Meatballs)

Istanbul Culinary Institute -Banu Özden

Preparation:

1. In a large bowl, mix all of the ingredients except the olive oil with your hands for about 10 minutes, until all ingredients are well blended and hold together.
2. Use a tablespoon of the meat mixture to form a oval sized small patty. Repeat until you have 30 patties and arrange in rows on a tray.
3. Cover and refrigerate for one hour.
4. Brush the barbeque or grill pan with olive oil and cook the meatballs until grilled to taste.
5. If you're using a non-stick frying pan instead, heat some olive oil and cook the köfte in batches making certain not to overcrowd. Keep the cooked batches hot in a warm oven until you're done.

Ingredients: (serves 6)

- 1 kg ground veal
- 1 large onion, grated, with juice
- 1 egg
- 2 cloves garlic, finely chopped
- 1 tbsp salt
- 1 ½ tsp black pepper
- 1 cup breadcrumbs
- 1 bunch basil, leaves only
- 3 tbsp olive oil
- Olive oil, enough to fry meatballs

Leek Köfte (Meatballs)

Lâle Apa - (recipe supplied by Arzu Akkoyunlu)

Preparation:

1. Cut the leeks into thin slices. Boil until tender, drain, squeeze to remove all excess water and leave to cool.
2. Combine ground beef, 1 of the eggs, salt and black pepper. Knead and let the mixture rest for 5-10 minutes.
3. Heat the corn oil on high heat in a heavy frying pan.
4. Shape the meat into small (5-cm) patties. Beat the remaining egg in a small bowl. Coat each meatball in flour and then dip into the beaten egg.
5. Fry the meatballs, remove and place on a paper towel to absorb excess oil.
6. The meatballs can be served hot or cold.

Chef's note:

Leek meatballs can be kept in the refrigerator for up to 3 days. They can be served as a finger food or on a bed of julienned sau sautéed leeks.

Ingredients: (serves 6)

- 1 kg leeks
- 300 g ground veal
- 2 eggs
- Corn oil, to fry meatballs
- Salt, to taste
- Black Pepper, to taste
- Flour, to coat meatballs

Lamb Shanks

Mehmet Gök – Four Seasons Hotel Sultanahmet

Preparation:

1. Sauté the shanks in a large pot with onion, garlic, celery stalk and leeks. Add tomato paste and water and bring to a boil. Reduce heat, add prunes and simmer for 2½ hours.
2. Remove prunes from pot, remove the pits and puree in a food processor.
3. Once the shanks have cooled, remove from bone and dice the meat.
4. Strain the cooking liquid in a sieve.
5. Simmer the stock on low heat for 4 hours.
6. Strain once again in a mesh strainer or cheese cloth and refrigerate.
7. The following day, skim the fat off the stock and boil for at least 3 hours without adding any herbs or spices. Continue boiling until the stock is reduced and has thickened.
8. Use a piping bag with a fluted tip to shape a bed of aubergine puree on each plate.
9. Combine the meat, fresh walnuts, 1 tablespoon butter, 1-2 tablespoons stock reduction and 1 sprig finely chopped oregano.
10. Place a ring mould over the aubergine puree and fill it to one-third with the lamb. Spoon the heated prune puree over the lamb. Remove the ring mould. Drizzle a little stock reduction over the aubergine puree.
11. Serve the rest of the lamb stock reduction in a gravy dish.

Preparation of aubergine puree:

1. Grill the aubergines over an open flame or in a hot oven, turning occasionally, for 5-6 minutes, depending on their size, until the skin is charred.
2. When the flesh is tender, grip the stem while still hot and strip off the charred skin. Cut off the stems.
3. Melt butter in a saucepan and sauté flour until it begins to turn golden brown. Add the aubergine and continue to sauté, stirring constantly for five minutes. Gradually add the warm milk, stirring constantly to prevent lumps. Force the mixture through a strainer with large holes.
4. Season with nutmeg, salt and black pepper.

Ingredients: (serves 6)

- 6 lamb shanks
- 1 cup leeks, coarsely chopped
- 1 celery stalk
- 1 yellow onion
- 2 cloves garlic, crushed
- 1 tbsp tomato paste
- 1-2 sprigs oregano
- ¼ cup shelled fresh walnuts
- Herbs for garnish
- 5 lt water

For the prune puree:

- 20 prunes

For the Aubergine Puree:

- 8 aubergines
- 2 tbsp flour
- 1 cup milk, warm
- 1 tsp butter
- Nutmeg, to taste
- Salt, to taste
- Black Pepper, to taste

Desserts

Holiday Halvah with Almonds and Caramel Sauce

Sevim Gökyıldız

Preparation:

1. Reserve 2 tablespoons of the sugar.
2. Combine milk, remaining sugar and vanilla powder in a saucepan and bring to a boil for 2 minutes. Allow to cool.
3. Soak almonds in boiling hot water for 10 minutes, then peel.
4. Melt butter in a saucepan. Add almonds and sauté until roasted.
5. Add the semolina, reduce to low heat and stir continuously for 30-35 minutes until almonds are totally roasted. When the semolina is golden brown, add warm milk, stirring continuously.
6. Cover and simmer for about 45 minutes or until the liquid is completely absorbed.
7. Add the reserved 2 tablespoons of sugar. Place a gauze or cotton cloth over the pan, cover with a lid and turn off the heat. Allow to stand for 15-20 minutes.
8. Spoon the halvah into a serving dish. Drizzle with the caramel sauce, sprinkle with nuts and candied fruit, and serve.

Preparation of the caramel sauce:

1. In a saucepan, on medium heat, add water and then stir in the sugar, and reduce heat to low.
2. When the mixture is golden , add cream and continue to stir rigorously and remove from heat.

Ingredients: (serves 6)

- 500 g / 3 ⅓ cup semolina
- 100 g / 1 cup almonds
- 300 g / 1 ½ cups sugar
- 4 cups milk
- 1 sachet vanilla powder
- 200 g / ¾ cups butter or margarine

For the caramel sauce:

- 200 g / 1 cup sugar
- 20 g / 3 tbsp water
- 100 ml / ⅓ cup heavy cream

Toppings:

- Dried figs, pistachios, hazelnuts, almonds and assorted candied fruit

Chef's note:

If desired, the halvah can be spooned into moulds, then turned over onto individual plates and served.

Şekerpare (Mini cakes with Syrup)

Istanbul Culinary Institute - Feyza Bayrakçıoğlu

Preparation:

1. To make the syrup, bring water and confectionary sugar to a boil and cook until the sugar is completely dissolved. Stir in the lemon juice. Put aside and allow it to cool.
2. Make the dough by blending the flour, margarine, coconot flakes, butter, confectionery sugar, baking soda, baking powder and eggs in a food processor.
3. Knead the dough for a few minutes on a clean counter. Form the dough into round balls a bit larger than a walnut. Arrange on a baking tray and lightly press down on each one to flatten. Place a hazelnut in the middle of each one.
4. Bake in a preheated oven for 5 minutes at 120°C/240°F. Increase the heat to 170°C/340°F and bake until golden brown.
5. Remove from oven and pour the cold syrup over the mini cakes. Wait for them to cool and absorb the syrup.
6. After 1-2 hours, spoon a little of the syrup onto a serving dish and dust with some ground pine nuts. Place the cakes on top of the syrup and serve at room temperature.

Chef's note:

Leftover şekerpare should be refrigerated.

Ingredients: (30 mini cakes)

- 1 kg flour
- 250 g margarine or butter
- 60 g / ¾ cup coconut flakes
- 200 g / 1 cup confectionery sugar
  1 ½ tsp baking soda
- 2 ¼ tsp baking powder
- 4 eggs
- 75 g / 24 hazelnuts, shelled

For the syrup:
- 1 kg sugar
- 5 ½ cups water
- ½ lemon, juice of
- Pine nuts, for garnish

Lemon Blancmange
(Adapted from 15th century recipe)

Marianna Yeraşimos

Preparation:

1. Thoroughly wash the lemons and pat dry. Grate the peel and reserve for later use. Juice the lemons into a separate bowl (¾ cup juice).

2. Pour the confectionery sugar in a pot. Sift and then add Maizena cornstarch and mix thoroughly. Stirring continuously, add lemon juice and water. When the mixture has dissolved, turn on the heat.

3. Cook, stirring continuously, until the mixture thickens. When it begins to bubble, cook for an additional 2-3 minutes.

4. Stir in 4 teaspoons of the grated lemon peel and turn off the heat.

5. Moisten the bottom of a 15x25cm dish with a few drops of water and pour the mixture into the dish. Cool at room temperature, and then chill in the refrigerator for 3-4 hours.

6. Remove from refrigerator and place the blancmange on a serving dish. Sprinkle with the remaining lemon zest and serve.

Ingredients: (serves 6)

- 2 large juicy lemons
- 8 tbsp confectionery sugar
- 3 tbsp Maizena cornstarch
- 2 cups water

Chef's note:

The cooling flavor of lemon and the lightness of the blancmange are the perfect combination for a summer dessert. Oranges can be used instead of lemons, but reduce the amount of confectionery sugar used accordingly. The blancmange can also be sprinkled with blanched almonds or unsalted fresh pistachios, and garnished with slices of fruit.

Homemade Cherry and Coriander Lokum (Turkish Delight)

Changa Restaurant

Preparation:

1. Puree the cherries in a blender or food processor and then place in a pot and bring to a boil.
2. Combine 60 g of confectionery sugar, glucose and pectin and gradually stir into the puree.
3. Dissolve the remaining confectionery sugar and pectin in the puree.
4. Thin the cornstarch with a bit of water and stir into the mixture.
5. Cook on high heat until the mixture begins to thicken. Lower heat and stir constantly until the mixture has fully thickened.
6. Stir in the coriander seeds. Pour the mixture onto a silicone or marble surface.
7. Once the mixture has cooled and thickened, cut into bite-size pieces.

Ingredients: (Serves 6)

- 450 g fresh cherries, pitted
- 450 g / 2 ¼ cups confectionery sugar
- 50 g / 6 tbsp cornstarch
- 30 g glucose
- 12 g pectin
- 50 g coriander seeds

Ahköekakan (Walnut and Chestnut Dessert)

Zeynep Çelikkan Kakınç

Preparation:

1. Crumble the walnuts with your hands or in a food processor. In a saucepan, sauté walnuts in butter for two minutes.
2. Remove the pan from the heat and allow the walnuts to cool. Add candied chestnuts and cream and mix well.
3. Spoon into single serving moulds. When cool, turn over onto individual serving dishes.
4. Drizzle with pekmez, cream or honey, and serve.

Ingredients: (serves 6)

- 1 kg crumbled candied chestnuts (preferably the Kafkas brand)
- 3 cups walnuts, shelled
- 150 ml / ½ cup cream
- 120 g / 8 tbsp butter

For the sauce:

- Pekmez (grape molasses), cream or honey.

Pumpkin Tatin with Pistachio Ice Cream

Mike Norman

Preparation:

1. Cut pumpkin into medium sized rounds and arrange in an oven tray.
2. Cover with sugar, cinnamon, cloves, walnuts and butter. Bake at 120°C /240°F for 25 minutes or until "al dente".
3. Once cool, remove pumpkin from the oven tray. Reserve the walnut syrup to use as the sauce in step 9.
4. Wrap each pumpkin round in a piece of mille-feuille pastry.
5. Brush the pastry-wrapped pumpkin with egg yolk and refrigerate for an hour.
6. Bake in a preheated oven 180°C/350°F oven until golden brown.
7. To plate, spoon Crème Anglaise sauce onto a serving dish.
8. Place the baked pumpkin over the sauce.
9. Drizzle with caramelized walnut sauce.
10. Serve with a scoop of pistachio ice cream.

Preparation of the Créme Anglaise:

1. In a small, heavy saucepan, heat cream and vanilla until bubbles form at the edges.
2. While cream is heating, whisk together egg yolks and sugar until smooth. Slowly pour ½ cup of hot milk mixture into egg yolks while constantly whisking.
3. Gradually add egg yolk mixture back to the remaining milk mixture while constantly whisking.
4. While constantly stirring, continue to cook until the mixture cots the back of a spoon.

Ingredients for Créme Anglaise:

- 1 cup heavy cream
- 2 tsp vanilla extract
- 4 egg yolks
- ⅓ cup white sugar

Ingredients: (serves 6)

- 1 kg pumpkin, peeled
- 1 kg mille-feuille pastry
- 1 egg yolk
- 500 g / 2 ¾ cups brown sugar
- 2 large cinnamon sticks
- 4 cloves
- 100 g / 6 ½ tbsp butter
- 50 g / ⅓ cup walnuts, roughly chopped
- 300 g pistachio ice cream
- 120 ml / ½ cup Crème Anglaise, available in markets in USA and Europe

Dates and Figs Dessert

Borsa Restaurant

Preparation:

1. Cut each fig into six pieces.
2. Pit and quarter the dates.
3. In a saucepan, simmer milk, heavy cream, dates and figs for 30-40 minutes or until the liquid is absorbed.
4. Cut each walnut into 3 pieces and add to the mixture.
5. When the mixture has thickened sufficiently, pour it in six moulds.
6. For the sponge cake, whisk the eggs and sugar in a bain marie (double boiler). When thoroughly heated, mix in a food processor for 3 minutes.
7. Sift flour and corn starch into a mixing bowl. Slowly stir in the whisked eggs.
8. Stir in the melted butter.
9. Pour the mixture into a cake pan and bake for approximately 25 minutes at 180°C/350°F.
10. Divide the sponge cake into six portions.
11. Put two spoonfuls of the fig and date mixture on each piece of cake. Decorate with the fruit garnish, either on top or to the side. Serve with a scoop of vanilla ice cream.

Ingredients: (serves 6)

- 300 g / 1 ½ cup dried figs
- 300 g / 1 ½ cups dates
- 300 ml / 1 cup heavy cream
- 300 ml / 1 ½ cups milk
- 100 g / ¾ cup walnuts, shelled
- 300 g vanilla ice cream

For the sponge cake:
- 5 eggs
- 10 egg yolks
- 300 g / 1 ½ cups sugar
- 200 g / 1 ⅔ cup flour
- 150 g / 1 ¼ cups corn starch
- 50 g / 3 tbsp butter, melted

For decoration:
- 25 g / 2 tbsp currants
- 25 g / 2 tbsp seedless raisins
- 25 g / 3 dried apricots

(The night before, boil raisins and apricots in ¼ cup water. Immediately remove from heat and allow to cool. Chop the apricots before garnishing)

Quince Puree

Istanbul Culinary Institute

Preparation:

1. Peel and remove core and seeds from the quinces.
2. Drop them into a bowl of acidulated water (2 tablespoons lemon juice per 4 cups of water)
3. Wrap the quince seeds in a small cheesecloth and tie.
4. Quarter the quinces and place them in a large pot.
5. Fill the pot with enough water to cover the fruit. Add sugar and the cheesecloth bundle of quince seeds. Bring to the boil.
6. Add cinnamon and cloves.
7. Cook until tender.
8. Remove the cheese cloth with seeds. Puree the remaing mixture in a food processor or blender and pour into a shallow dish. Can be stored in the refrigerator for several days.
9. To serve as an hors-d'oeuvre, simply spread some pureed quince and blue cheese on crostini.

Chef's note:

Alternatively, once the quince puree has set, it can be cut into cubes and sprinkled over arugula (rocket) or green salad.

Ingredients: (serves 6)

- 6 quince, peeled
- 2 ½ cups sugar
- Water, as required
- ½ tsp clove, ground
- ½ tsp cinnamon
- 1 lemon

Sesame Apricots

Sevim Gökyıldız

Preparation:

1. Soak apricots overnight in just enough water to cover them.
2. Drain apricots and place in a pot.
3. Add sugar and lemon juice and simmer covered on low heat for about 10 minutes.
4. Remove the lid and continue cooking until the liquid has thickened to the consistency of syrup. As a result, apricots will plump up and the sesame seeds will stick to the apricots when you serve them.
5. Spoon the apricots onto a serving dish and allow to them cool.
6. Fill the apricots with clotted cream. Roast sesame seeds in a non-stick frying pan for a few minutes and sprinkle over the apricots.
7. Serve cold.

Ingredients: (serves 6)

- 500 g dried apricots
- 150 g sugar
- ¾ cup of water
- 1 tsp lemon juice
- 50 g / 1 tbsp sesame seeds, roasted
- clotted cream, as needed

Candied Pumpkin

Sevim Gökyıldız

Preparation:

1. Peel the pumpkin, cut into 6cm slices and place in a large pot.
2. Add ¾ cup water and butter. Cover and simmer, occasionally adding water if necessary.
3. When the pumpkin begins to soften, add the sugar.
4. Continue simmering for about 45 minutes or until the pumpkin is tender, glossy and slightly caramelized.
5. Plate, sprinkle with walnuts and top with a dollop of clotted cream.

Ingredients: (serves 6)

- 1 kg pumpkin
- 400 g / 2 cups sugar
- 100 g / ¾ cups walnuts, diced
- 1 heaping tbsp butter
- 200 ml / ¾ cup water
- Clotted cream, as desired

Güllabiye Halvah

Dr. Özge Samancı

Preparation:

1. Heat honey in a wide pot.
2. Stir in butter and remove from the heat.
3. Combine maizena and 150 ml of the water to form a paste. Add the remaining water.
4. Slowly stir the honey into the maizena paste mixture and mix well. Add almonds and rosewater and return to the heat.
5. Heat on medium until the mixture thickens.
6. Pour the halvah onto a small tray.
7. Once cool, cut into squares, garnish with almonds and serve.

Chef's note:

Halvah (helva in Turkish), is a dessert typically prepared with either semolina or nut butter (a spreadable foodstuff prepared with crushed nuts - i.e. peanut, walnut, etc.) and was a staple in Ottoman cooking. Although this recipe is adapted from an anonymous cookbook published in Istanbul in 1880, its origins go back much further. Contemporary Turkish cuisine no longer features the medieval combination of rosewater and musk once popular in Middle Eastern desserts and that gives this halvah its distinctive flavor.

To use musk in this recipe, crush a piece of musk the size of a pea and dissolve in rosewater. The musk used in Ottoman cooking was obtained from an Asian deer, native to the high mountains of Asia. Nearly all of the musk used today is synthetic.

Ingredients: (serves 6)

- 300 g / 1 cup honey
- 100 g / 6 tbsp butter
- 250 g / 2 cups maizena or wheat starch
- 450 ml / 1 ¾ cup water
- 50 g / ⅓ cup almonds, blanched and roasted
- 2 tsp rosewater
- Musk, optional

Rose Petal Pudding

Gönül Paksoy

Preparation:

1. 4-5 hours before preparing the pudding, rub the rose petals with half of the sugar and refrigerate.
2. Place the rose petals in a pot, add water and cook, stirring occasionally, until the consistency of a sauce is reached. Add lemon juice and allow to cool.
3. In a separate pot, mix the milk and rice flour, ensuring that there are no lumps. Cook on medium heat until it comes to a boil, continuously stirring in the same direction.
4. Lower the heat and simmer until it thickens. Add the rest of the sugar, adjusting the amount to taste.
5. Cook for an additional 4-5 minutes. Then add poppy seeds and labne cheese and stir rigorously stir.
6. After a few minutes of stirring, add the dried petals, making sure they are evenly dispersed. Pour into a serving bowl, drizzle with the rose petal sauce and serve.

Ingredients: (serves 6)

* ½ cup food quality fresh rose petals
* ¾ cup water
* 1 tsp lemon juice
* 2 cups milk
* ¼ cup rice flour
* ¾ cup sugar
* 1 tbsp poppy seeds
* 200 g labne cheese
* 2 tbsp dried rose petals

Citrus Pudding with Cherry Sauce

Deniz Alphan

Preparation:

Preparation of the cherry sauce:

1. In a saucepan, dissolve cornstarch and sugar in half a cup of water. Simmer on medium heat with the cherries until the mixture thickens.
2. Refrigerate until you're ready to serve the pudding.
3. If desired, add a splash of Grand Marnier or cherry liqueur.

Preparation of the pudding:

1. Melt margarine in a saucepan. Add flour and sauté lightly.
2. Add sugar, melt and simmer, stirring continuously, until the mixture thickens to the texture of a pudding.
3. Stir in the orange juice, grated orange peel and vanilla.
4. Blend with a mixer for 10 minutes and pour into individual serving bowls.
5. Chill in the refrigerator for 6 hours, then spoon the cherry sauce on top and serve.

Ingredients: (serves 6)

- 200 g / 1 ¼ cups margarine
- ½ cup flour
- ½ cup sugar
- 1 package vanilla
- 1 lt milk
- 1 medium orange, juice and grated peel

For the cherry sauce:

- 250 g / 1 ⅔ cups cherries, pitted, fresh or frozen
- 1 tbsp cornstarch
- ½ cup water
- 3 tbsp sugar

Fig Pudding

Hülya Ekşigil

Preparation:

1. Slice the stems off the figs and cut into quarters.
2. Slowly heat the milk and brown sugar in a saucepan over low heat until the sugar is dissolved. The milk should be lukewarm.
3. Puree the sweetened milk, figs and cinnamon in a food processor.
4. Set aside 6 walnut halves. Chop the remaining walnuts and add to the fig mixture.
5. Pour into individual dessert bowls.
6. Cover the bowls with plastic wrap and place them on a tray and cover with a towel. Allow them to cool down for 4 hours at room temperature.
7. Then put the dessert in the refrigerator and thoroughly chill.
8. Garnish each portion with half a walnut and serve.

Chef's note:

This dessert, which was created long before the concept of "healthy eating" had been conceived, is as nutritious as it is delicious. Lightly roast the walnuts before adding them to the pudding if you'd like a stronger flavor.

Ingredients: (serves 6)

- ½ lt milk
- ¼ cup brown sugar
- 8 dried figs
- 10-12 fresh walnuts, shelled
- 1 ½ tsp cinnamon

Halvah with Halloumi Cheese

Ümit Yüksel - Sheraton İstanbul Maslak Hotel

Preparation:

1. Melt butter in a small saucepan. Add flour and sauté on low heat for 10-15 minutes or until it begins to turn golden brown.
2. Prepare the syrup by boiling sugar, lemon juice and peel, and water for 15-20 minutes.
3. Carefully stir the syrup into the flour mixture in the other pan. Use a long-handle spoon to avoid being scalded by the syrup.
4. Cover, remove from the heat and allow the halvah mixture to sit for 15-20 minutes.
5. Stir the cheese into the halvah.
6. Firmly press the halvah into an individual mould or bowl and then turn over onto individual serving dishes.
7. Serve warm with a scoop of vanilla ice cream and a sprinkling of diced apricots and figs.

Ingredients: (serves 6)

- 9 tbsp butter
- 1 ²/₃ cups flour
- 50 g halloumi cheese, diced
- 1 cup sugar
- 1 cup water
- ½ lemon, juice and peel of
- 1-2 dried apricots, diced
- 1-2 dried figs, diced

Petaluda

Takuhi Tovmasyan Zaman

Preparation:

1. On a clean counter, pour the flour and make a well in the middle of the flour. Add salt, eggs and water. Knead and work the dough until the consistency is smooth and elastic.

2. Cover the dough with a towel and let it rest for an hour.

3. To make the sherbet, combine the sugar, water and lemon juice in a pot and bring to the boil, cooking until it reaches the desired consistency.

4. Grind a handful of walnuts in a mortar and pestle, and reserve for later use.

5. Divide the dough in half. Sprinkle each one with half a handful of flour and using a rollin pin, roll out on a flat surface to about 1mm thickness.

6. Then, cut the dough into pieces 10cm wide by 7cm long.

7. Cut the pieces in half so they are 5cm wide and 7cm long. Using the tip of a sharp knife, cut 5-6 parallel slits into each piece of dough, leaving the edges intact and about 1-cm of uncut dough at the top and bottom of each slit. You should end up with a 5cm x 7cm piece of dough with 5-6 "slits" that resemble the runs in a nylon stocking.

8. Pick up the piece of dough and begin weaving the slits as follows: Gently pull up the second slit and wind the first slit under and around it. Continue by weaving each of the remaining slits under and around the second slit, similar to like making a cat's cradle.. Firmly press down the final slit after you've woven it.

9. If you have difficulty weaving the dough as instructed above, cut the dough into 3cm x 5cm strips and curl into butterfly shapes.

10. Heat the sunflower oil in a deep pot. Meanwhile, keep the sherbet warm on extremely low heat.

11. Fry the strips of dough in the hot oil. They will sink to the bottom, changing color and expanding as it rises to the top. When it turns golden brown remove with a slotted spoon, drain excess oil and toss into the hot sherbet. After 1 minute, remove the pastry, drain excess sherbet and layer on a serving dish. Sprinkle ground walnuts on each layer and serve.

Ingredients: (serves 6)

- 1 egg
- 1 eggshell of water
- 1 pinch salt
- Flour, as required

For the sherbet:
- 1 ½ cups sugar
- 1 cup water
- 3-5 drops lemon juice

For frying:
- 2 cups sunflower oil

For garnish:
- 1 handful walnuts, ground

Pear Terrine with Basil Ice Cream and Cinnamon

Mehmet Gürs

Preparation:

Preparation of the Pear Terrine:

1. Peel the pears and cut into 2cm thick segments.
2. Soak the gelatine in cold water.
3. In a large pot, sauté the pear slices in butter until the edges begin to change color and they soften slightly.
4. Remove the pears and discard any butter left in the pot.
5. Return the pear slices to the pot and add sugar. Cook on medium heat until caramelized.
6. Gently stir in aniseed and gelatine until evenly distributed.
7. Gentle pour the mixture onto a baking tray and allow it to cool slightly.
8. Tightly pack into a non-stick terrine mould when cool enough to handle.
9. Cover and refrigerate for 24 hours.

Preparation of the Basil Ice Cream:

1. Whisk egg yolks, sugar and honey until frothy.
2. Meanwhile, heat the milk and cream to 85°C/185°F.
3. Add the egg mixture to the hot milk and cream, whisking constantly until the temperature reaches 75°C/ 165°F.
4. Soak the gelatine sheets in cold water.
5. Pour the mixture into in a bowl placed in an ice bath and cook quickly.
6. Add the vodka.
7. Transfer 1 liter of the ice cream mixture and the basil into a blender and pulse until the basil is evenly dispersed.
8. Return the basil mixture to the bowl, add the soaked gelatine and mix.
9. Churn in an ice cream maker.

Chef's note:

100 grams of terrine is sufficient per portion. Leftovers can be kept for 2 days. The best variety of pear for this recipe is "Deveci", a crisp, juicy and sweet Anatolian pear that weighs about 350-400 grams.

Preparation of the Cinnamon Cookie Crumbs:

1. Mix all ingredients in a food processor fitted with a steel blade.
2. Spread out mixture on a cookie sheet and bake for 15 minutes at 180˚C/350˚F.
3. By hand, crumble the toasted mixture into small crumbs.
4. Cool and store in an airtight container until service.

Just before serving:

1. Cut the Pear Terrine into 1-cm slices.
2. Brush the terrine with some of the thinned gelatine and wait for it to set.
3. Serve the terrine with a scoop of ice cream topped with a tiny heap of cookie crumbs.

Ingredients: (serves 6)

Ingredients for the Pear Terrine:
- 4 kg pears
- 125 g / 8 tbsp clarified butter
- 500 g / 2 ½ cups caster/superfine sugar
- 45 g gelatine, sheet
- 15 g / 1 tbsp ground aniseed

Ingredients for the Cinnamon Cookie Crumbs:
- 100 g / ¾ cup flour
- 100 g / ¾ cup almonds, ground
- 100 g / 6 ½ tbsp cold butter
- 100 g / ½ cup sugar
- 20 g / 4 tsp cinnamon, ground

Ingredients for the Basil Ice Cream:
- 1 lt / 4 cups whole milk
- 1 lt / 4 cups heavy cream
- 450 g egg yolks
- 500 g / 2 ½ cups caster/superfine sugar
- 200 g / ⅔ cup honey
- 5 g gelatine, sheet
- 6 cl / ¼ cup vodka
- 100 g / ¾ cup fresh basil leaves

Candied Pumpkin Wrapped in Kadayıf and served with Tahini and Grape Molasses (Pekmez) Sauce

Ümit Yüksel - Sheraton İstanbul Maslak Hotel

Preparation:

1. Divide the pumpkin in quarters, peel and scoop out seeds. Cut into squares, arrange on a baking tray and sprinkle with sugar. Leave for 1-2 hours, until the pumpkin begins to "sweat".

2. Once pumpkin sweats, cover with aluminium foil and bake in oven at 180-200°C/350-375°F for 2.5 hours.

3. Allow pumpkin to cool and then wrap them in the kadayıf pastry. Put them back on the tray and bake at 180°C/350°F until the kadayıf turns golden brown.

4. Combine the tahini and grape molasses (pekmez).

5. Cut the pumpkin quarters in half and arrange on a serving dish that has been drizzled with the tahini and pekmez sauce.

6. Garnish with ground walnuts.

Alternative Method:

A calcium hydroxide bath (also known as 'pickling lime', 'hydrated lime' and 'slaked lime') gives the pumkin a crunchy texture and helps it retain its shape in this alternative recipe:

1. Add a couple of tablespoons of slaked lime to a liter of water.

2. Peel and remove the pumpkin's seeds. Cut into quarters and then into square pieces. Place the pieces into the lime water.

3. In a seperate pot, bring 750 ml water and 2 cups sugar to a boil and simmer for 15-20 minutes. Drain the pumpkin pieces and simmer in this syrup for 30-45 minutes, until the skin is crunchy and the flesh soft.

4. Remove the pumpkin from the pot. When cool enough to work with, wrap each piece in kadayıf pastry and bake in the oven at 180°C/350°F until golden brown. Cut the baked pumpkin pieces in half and serve with pekmez and tahini sauce, topped with ground walnuts.

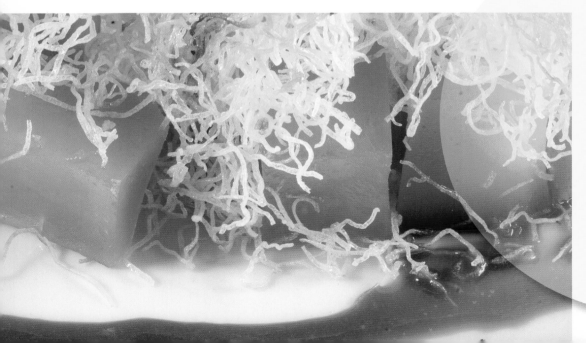

Chef's note:

Kadayıf is long strands of pastry, similar in look to shredded wheat. In Turkey, it's usually used to make desserts with hot syrup, clotted cream, nuts or cheese.

Ingredients: (serves 6)

- 100 g. **kadayıf pastry**
- 1.2 kg pumpkin or butternut squash
- 2 cups sugar
- ½ cup tahini
- ½ cup grape pekmez (grape molasses)
- 1 ½ tablespoons walnuts, ground

Sütlü Zerde (Milky Zerde)

Asitane Restaurant

Preparation:

1. Moisten saffron in rosewater until it begins to dissolve and change color.
2. In a pot, bring milk to the boil and add the rosewater and saffron mixture and then the sugar.
3. Remove any foreign objects from the rice and soak in water for 15 minutes. Drain and rinse well.
4. In a separate bowl, boil the rice in 1 cup of water. When the water has been absorbed and the rice has become a bit soft and mushy, add the hot milk and rosewater mixture. Simmer on low heat for a few minutes.
5. In a separate bowl, whisk rice flour, cornstarch, egg yolks and milk and add to the pot and simmer for an additional five minutes.
6. Pour into individual serving bowls, allow to cool and refrigerate.
7. Garnish with pine nuts and raisons and serve.

Ingredients: (serves 6)

- 1 pinch saffron
- 1 tbsp rosewater
- 4 cups milk
- 1 cup sugar
- ¼ cup rice
- 1 cup water
- Pine nuts and raisons, for garnish

For the thickener:
- 1 ½ tbsp rice flour
- 6 tbsp cornstarch
- 2 egg yolks
- ¾ cups milk

Pomegranate Blossom Sherbet

Asitane Restaurant

Preparation:

1. Soak pomegranate blossoms in water the night before serving.
2. In a large pot, boil in water and sugar on medium heat for 15 minutes.
3. Strain through fine mesh or cheesecloth and serve chilled.

Ingredients:

- 8 lt / 32 cups water
- 300 g pomegranate blossoms
- 1200 g / 6 cups sugar

Chef's note:

Can keep for up to 2-3 days in the refrigerator.

Cinnamon Sherbet

Asitane Restaurant

Preparation:

1. Grind cinnamon sticks and cloves in a mortar and pestle. Put the cinnamon and cloves in one cloth sachet and the chilli peppers in another.
2. Fill 2 pots with a cup of water each and place a sachet in each pot.
3. Boil the cinnamon and cloves sachet for 15 minutes and the chilli peppers sachet for 10 minutes and remove from heat.
4. When cool, squeeze the excess water from each sachet into their respective pots.
5. Measure the water in each pot, adding as much water as necessary to produce one cup of each liquid.
6. Pour the sugar into a separate pot. Add the cinnamon and pepper infused liquid and bring to a boil for about 10 minutes or until the sugar is completely dissolved and evenly dispersed.
7. Continue simmering until the liquid is reduced to a sherbert the thickness of honey.
8. Dissolve the citric acid in a little water and stir into the sherbert.
9. Pour into individual glasses and garnish with cinnamon sticks.

Chef's note:

Cinnamon sherbet is the primary ingredient for a sorbet, which can be prepared by placing the mixture in the freezer and stirring it with a fork 3 times every 30 minutes. It can be kept frozen for 2-3 months. In order to turn the frozen sherbet into a beverage, simply add hot water until reaches the desired consistency.

Ingredients: (serves 6)

- 2 cinnamon sticks
- 5 whole cloves
- 3 tbsp hot chilli peppers
- 2 ½ cups sugar
- 2 cups water
- 1 tsp citric acid
- Cinnamon stickes, for garnish

Strawberry and Wine Jello

İnci Birsel

Preparation:

1. Measure enough strawberry flavored gelatin package to get 4 cups of liquid.
2. Dissolve gelatin in one cup hot water and stir in the chilled wine.
3. Pour mixture into a shallow, large dish and chill until set (preferably overnight)
4. One hour before serving, wash, core and thinly slice the strawberries lenghtwise. Then toss strawberries with ¼ cup sugar. Chill until ready to serve dessert.
5. With a fork, break gelatin into small flakes and to make sure they are totally mixed. Spoon 3 tablespoons of gelatin into each serving glass and top with a layer of strawberry slices. Repeat two or more times with layers of gelatin and fruit.
6. Top with a dollop of whipped cream or a scoop of ice cream, garnish with chopped pistachio nuts and serve.

Chef's note:

If packaged strawberry jello is not available, dissolve 7-8 sheets of gelatin in a sufficient amount of cold water. Once dissolved, add 22.5cl boiled strawberry juice or 67.5cl strawberry wine. Refrigerate to set and then continue with Step 3.

Ingredients: (serves 6)

- 1 package strawberry jello
- 22.5 cl / 1 cup boiling water
- 67.5 cl / 3 cups chilled sweet or fruit wine (strawberry or cranberry)
- 500 g / ½ kg ripe strawberries
- 50 g / ¼ cup sugar
- Pistachio nuts, chopped, for garnish

Sahlep Pudding with Strawberries

Pierre Levy

Preparation:

1. To prepare the pudding, in a heavy saucepan, melt margarine and butter over low heat. Stir in the flour or rice flour until smooth. Ensure the color doesn't darken; the mixture should stay white or pale yellow.

2. Add milk and sahlep and continue to stir with a wooden spatula or spoon over low heat until the mixture thickens and is fully cooked.

3. Pour the hot pudding into 8-cm bowls or moulds and leave to cool, uncovered, on a tray. When cool, cover the bowls with plastic wrap and refrigerate until you're ready to serve.

4. To prepare the strawberry syrup, rinse and core strawberries. In a saucepan, simmer on low heat until they reach the consistency of syrup. Force the strawberry mixture through a strainer when fully cooked. You should have about half a cup of strawberry syrup. Let the syrup cool.

5. Core the strawberries reserved for garnish and cut into thin slices.

6. Layer the slices over the pudding so they overlap slightly and place on whole strawberry in the center. Brush the syrup over the strawberries to make them glisten and garnish with ground pistachio nuts.

Chef's note:

If you wish, serve with ice cream or wild strawberries.

Ingredients: (serves 6)

For the pudding:
- 8 tbsp margarine
- 8 tbsp pasteurized butter
- ½ cup flour
- ⅓ cup rice flour (if using white flour, 1 cup water)
- 1 tbsp sahlep flour, adjusted for desired thickness
- 4 cups whole milk
- Pistachio nuts, ground, for garnish

For the strawberry syrup:
- ½ kg fresh strawberries
- 2 tbsp sugar

For garnish:
- 18 -20 fresh, ripe strawberries

185

Macaroons with Pomegranate and Beetroot Ganache

Pierre Levy

Preparation:

1. For the puree, boil beetroots in water until tender the day before you make the macaroons. Peel, remove roots and puree. Leave overnight in cheesecloth to strain excess liquid.

2. For the beetroot powder, cut 1 medium beetroot into paper-thin slices and bake in a preheated oven at 50-70°C/130-150°F or sun-dry until completely dry. Grind the beet into a powder and use it as a natural food coloring for the macaroons, as needed. If you prefer to skip this step use store bought food coloring, but be careful to use only as much as needed.

3. To make the cookies, begin by whisking the egg whites in a bowl. Add sugar before the mixture hardens and continue whisking until the sugar has been dissolved.

4. With a sieve, sift the ground almonds and confectionery sugar into a bowl.

5. Slowly stir the sugar and almond mixture into the beaten egg whites, which will lose some of their volume. Immediately put this mixture into a pastry bag and pipe your cookies onto a baking tray lined with grease paper or a silicone mat. Make sure you have an even amount of cookies. Bake in a preheated oven for 10 minutes at 130-140°C/265-285° or until the exterior of the cookies are crisp while the insides are still soft.

6. To make the ganache, break white chocolate into small pieces and melt in a double-boiler, stirring constantly.

7. When the chocolate has melted, stir in pomegranate syrup, beetroot puree and mascarpone cheese until thoroughly mixed.

8. Fill a pastry bag with the ganache and pipe a dollop of the filling into half of the cookies. Cover each with another cookie and slightly pressing down on each one to sandwhich and create your macaroon.

Chef's note:

The macaroons can be refrigerated in an air-tight sealed container for a few days or frozen for up to two weeks. If you make the cookies in advance, they keep in the refrigerator for up to a month.

Ingredients: (serves 6)
- 200 g beetroot

For the cookies:
- 150 g egg white
- 62 g / 5 tbsp sugar
- Beet powder (as required)
- 150 g / 1 ½ cups almonds, finely ground
- 312 g / 3 cups + 2 tbsp confectionery sugar

For the ganache:
- 200 g white chocolate
- 20 g / 1 tbsp pomegranate syrup (or reduced balsamic vinegar)
- 80 g / ⅔ cup beet puree
- 150 g mascarpone

Frigo Pudding

Istanbul Culinary Institute

Preparation:

1- With a sieve, sift rice flour, cornstarch, flour, stir in sugar and mix.
2- Whisk together the eggs and milk and pout into the dry ingredients. Bring to a boil, stirring constantly. When the mixture thickens, stir in the butter and remove from heat.
3- Pour the mixture into a shallow container or individual dessert bowls. Place in the refrigerator for 2 hours.
4- Just before serving, sprinkle with ground pistachios or hazelnuts.

Chef's note:

Alternatively, nuts can be stirred into the mixture before chilling.

Ingredients: (serves 6)

- 2 tbsp unsweetened cocoa powder
- 2 tbsp rice flour
- 2 tbsp cornstarch
- 4 tbsp flour
- 1 ¾ cup sugar
- 2 eggs
- 1 lt milk
- 2 tbsp butter

Chefs

Asitane Restaurant
Batur Durmay

Under the Ottoman Empire, the guilds of cooks kept their recipes and culinary techniques a closely guarded secret, with master chefs passing along their reipes and techniques to their apprentices verbally. Even so, Asitane Restaurant has succeeded in recreating many of those long-lost Ottoman dishes, thereby creating an incomparable dining experience.

The menu at Asitane Restaurant was developed after months of extensive research that involved scouring palace archives for the few surviving imperial kitchen registries. Since its opening in 1990, these original sources have served as the foundation for over 200 long-forgotten savory and sweet Ottoman dishes.

Located in the Old City just off a tranquil square lined with beautifully restored wooden houses, Asitane Restaurant stands in the shadows of Chora Church, which today is a public museum housing some of the finest Byzantine mosaics and frescoes in the world.

Kariye Camii Sokak, No. 6
Edirnekapı 34240 İstanbul
Tel: +90 212 635 79 97
Fax: +90 212 521 66 31
www.asitanerestaurant.com
info@asitanerestaurant.com

Aret Sahakyan

Before becoming the manager and executive chef at Cities, one of the trendiest resturants of its time in Washington DC, Aret Sahakyan worked other prestigious Washington establishments to include Toskana, Ricchi, Jean-Louis Palladin, Pavillion and Gallelio, all 2 Michelin star restaurants.

The original concept of Cities was to completely change the menu and cuisine every six months. As a result, Sahakyan visited 12 cities to gather ideas and recipes. As he traveled throughout the Mediterranean, his fascination with the regional dishes inspired him to incorporate local cooking techniques into his own culinary repertoire. Sahakyan later returned to Turkey, He uses only the finest locally grown ingredients and olive oils at Maça Kızı, his restaurant in the Aegean resort town of Bodrum. Along with close friend Sahir Erozan, Sahakyan had also ventured into the Istanbul fine dining scene, when he assumed the position of executive chef at Tuus, which opened its doors in 2006 .

In 2009, Sahakyan's intense passion for Mediterranean cuisine led him to Spain, where he traveled extensively researching tapas dishes, his personal interpretation of which is now served at Maça Kızı in the form of appetizers using local ingredients.

aret@macakizi.com

Beyti Güler
Beyti Restaurant

Although much has changed since 1945 when Beyti Restaurant opened in the Küçükçekmece district of Istanbul with jıust 4 tables and seating for 16, the family's dedication to exceptional service and quality has been kept alive down the generations.

Today, at its spacious 3000-square-meter premises in Florya, with a seating capacity for 600 spread out over 3 garden patios and 11 "salons" inspired by Ottoman-Turkish architecture, Beyti Restaurant is still, in the words of Lord Kinross, "the best place to eat meat in all of Europe". In order to maintain the exceptional quality for which it is renowned, Beyti continues to procure and age its own meat.

In terms of its cuisine, attentive staff, décor and garden, Beyti Restaurant is an Istanbul institution in a category all its own.

Orman Sokak No. 8 Florya, İstanbul
Tel:: +90 212 663 29 90
bilgi@beyti.com.tr

Borsa Restaurant
Mustafa Baylan

Established in 1927 in the Bahçekapı district of Istanbul, Borsa Restaurant took its name from the Zahire Borsası (Produce Exchange) located nearby. After relocating to Sirkeci in 1983, the restaurant was sold to 3 brothers: Rasim, Tahsin and Ali Reşat Özkanca. The brothers expanded their a la carte, white tablecloth restaurant by opening a chain of centrally located, self-service cafeterias serving traditional Turkish dishes.

Over the years, Borsa Catering has provided its services at numerous international meetings and cultural events held at the Atatürk Cultural Center between1993 and 2007; at the Lütfi Kırdar International Convention and Exhibition Centrer since 1996; and at the Sakıp Sabancı Educational and Cultural Center–Âdile Sultan Palace, since 2006. Borsa currently has four restaurants: Boğaziçi Borsa Restaurant in Harbiye, Borsa Restaurant in Kandilli, Borsa Restaurant at Istinye Park and the newly owned X Restaurant at Deniz Palas in Tepebaşı.

Lütfi Kırdar International Convention & Exhibition Center
Harbiye – Istanbul
Tel: +90 212 232 42 01
www.borsarestaurants.com
info@borsarestaurants.com

Changa Restaurant
Civan Er

Open since 1999, the menu at Changa, under the consultancy and supervision of renowned chef Peter Gordon, combines creative cooking techniques with ingredients from across the globe, while sister restaurant muzedechanga, located in the gardens of the Sabancı University Sakıp Sabancı Museum, also incorporates regional flavors and local tastes.

Sıraselviler Caddesi No. 47
Taksim 34433 İstanbul
www.changa-istanbul.com
changaistanbul@turk.net

Deniz Alphan

Deniz Alphan is the editorial director of the weekend supplements of Milliyet newspaper. The former editor of publications including the weekend supplements of Sabah newspaper and Vizyon magazine, Alphan is also the author of "Dina's Kitchen", a cookbook exploring Turkish-Sephardic cuisine.

Alphan was born in Istanbul and currently resides in the Büyükdere district.

GSM: + 90 532 674 02 76
ddalphan@gmail.com

Engin Akın

Described by the US based Food & Wine magazine as the Turkish version of Julia Child and Martha Stewart rolled up into one, Engin Akın is a world-renowned authority on Turkish cuisine. "Two Nations at the Same Table", a comparative study of Turkish and Greek cuisine she co-authored with Greek food writer Mirsini Lambarki, won the "Best Mediterranean Book" award at the Gourmand Book Awards in Barcelona in 2004. "Lezzetiye", a food and travel book in which Akın explores the cross-cultural influences of Turkish cuisine, was published by Albatros Publishing in 2007. She was featured in a ten-page spread in Food & Wine Magazine in 2001 and her recipes have appeared in international publications to include the San Francisco Chronicle, Los Angeles Times and Food Arts magazine. Additionally, Akın has contributed eight traditional Turkish dishes to the popular US based food magazine Bon Appétit and her recipes have appeared in other American publications including the New York Times. Her recipe for "Turkish Tomato Salad" was featured among the top 30 recipes over 30 years in the special 30th anniversary issue of Food & Wine Magazine. She has also participated in several culinary art performances at such venues as Gallery Apel and the Modern Art Museum in Luxembourg. Engin Akın's most recent cookbook , "From Tent to Palace – Turkish Cuisine", was published in Turkish and English by İş Bank Cultural Publications in the autumn of 2009.

engina03@mynet.com

Eyüp Kemal Sevinç
Founder, Hobimle Mutluyum Culinary Arts School

Eyüp Kemal Sevinç followed in his father's footsteps by becoming a chef in 1991. From the beginning and in a short period of time, he brought an innovativeness to Turkish cuisine and enjoyed great professional success. Eyüp Kemal Sevinç has had many "firsts". He was the winner of the first Turkish Culinary Competition in 1995; the first Turk to win a gold medal and the title "Best Young Chef of the Year" award at the International Culinary Competition, held in London in 1996; and the first member of the Turkish National Culinary Team, which was founded that same year. Sevinç regularly appears on nationally televised cooking programs and has won over 100 medals, cups and awards at national and international competitions. Since 2001, he has also served on the international juries of professional culinary competitions and as an expert juror for competitions in Turkey featuring regional dishes. Sevinç has helped promote Turkish tourism by introducing Turkish Cuisine to international audiences in numerous countries. He served as the Chairman of the Turkish National Culinary Team until 2007, the year in which he was named Istanbul Marriott Hotel Asia Executive Chef, a position he held until November 2009. Eyüp Kemal Sevinç established Hobimle Mutluyum Culinary Arts School in June 2009.

Kalamış Fener Caddesi, Kılıç Sokak No. 3/2
Fenerbahçe-Kadıköy, Istanbul
GSM: + 90 532 346 06 78
www.eyupsevinc.com
chefeyup@eyupsevinc.com.

Gökçen Adar

After Izmir-born Gökçen Adar retired from a career as a mechanical engineer in 1992, he turned his attention and culinary experience to writing cookbooks and oprganizing exhibitions. During his extensive research into the cuisines of İzmir and the Aegean region, he began collecting recipes for traditional dishes that were in danger of being forgotten.

Adar has traveled throughout Anatolia collecting over 5,000 recipes and has compiled one of the most comprehensive food archives in Turkey. He is also passionate about handicrafts. A typical day involves tending his garden where he grows a wide variety of herbs,and spending two to three hours each day painting and writing books. Books he has authored include "The Tastes of the Aegean", "From the Taurus Mountains to the Mediterranean: the Flavors of Antalya", "Four Seasons in the Kitchen", "Turquoise Blue", "The Flavors of Turkey", "The Scents of the Sea: 80 Unforgettable Recipes" and, most recently, "The Dance of Wild Greens and Olive Oil".

agadar2006@hotmail.com

Gönül Paksoy

Hülya Ekşigil

İnci Birsel

Born in Adana, where she completed her early education, Gönül Paksoy graduated from the Chemical Engineering department at Yıldız Technical University in Istanbul. Afterwards, she went on to earn an M.S. degree from Çukurova University in Adana for her paper on "The Separation of Tar Into Compounds and its Definition" and a Ph.D from the same university for her thesis on "The Use of Plants as a Source of Natural Dyes". Paksoy continued her research into natural dyes after she resigned from her university post in 1989. In addition to her ongoing research, Paksoy is a cutting-edge designer and an instructor at the Textiles and Fashion Design Department at the School of Fine Arts at Mimar Sinan University in Istanbul.

Her creations have been exhibited throughout Turkey and in numerous countries abroad.

In October 2005, Paksoy received a Smithsonian Freer Gallery of Art and Arthur M. Zagler design award for her designs incorporating science and art, the past and the future. Her published works include: "Culinary Designs I", "Rag Dolls", "From Collection to Creation: Gönül Paksoy I", "From Collection to Creation: Gönül Paksoy II", "Culinary Designs II".

gonulpaksoy@yahoo.com
gonulpaksoy@gmail.com
Tel: + 90 212 261 90 81
Tel: + 90 212 236 02 09

Following a long career in the magazine industry, Hülya Ekşigil made of a career out of what had previously been a hobby: writing about culinary culture. She now teaches university students about the magazine industry, but her own career in the media is limited to the articles she pens for magazines. Her professional forays into culinary arts have included a weekly televised cooking program and the editing of two cookbooks. Her own book, "My Tastebuds are Smiling!", is compiled from food articles she wrote over a six-year period. Hülya Ekşigil also prepared and presented the Istanbul episode of "Diary of a Foodie" aired on the National Geographic channel. Currently, she is preparing a guide book designed to make life easier for "those who think the kitchen is another planet".

heksigil@yahoo.com.tr

Born in İzmir in 1947, İnci Birsel spent a year of high school in the USA and graduated from the American College in Izmir in 1966. After completing her education, she began teaching at her alma mater American College in Izmir, got married and had two children. After Birsel retired in 1993 she drew on her culinary experience to author two cookbooks. İnci Birsel has been cooking full-time for 42 years and describes it as her greatest passion in life – along with her grandchildren.

www.mycookingnotebook.com
incibirsel@gmail.com

Kıyı Restaurant
Yorgi Sabuncu

An Istanbul culinary institution on the shores of the Bosphorus in Tarabya, Kıyı Restaurant has been serving fresh seafood and meze (appetizers) since 1966. Popular with expats and foreign guests, Kıyı has been named "Best Restaurant" by Hürriyet Newsapaper and Time Out Istanbul.

Kefeliköy Caddesi No. 126
Tarabya 80880 Istanbul
Tel: +90 212 262 00 02
www.kiyi.com.tr

Mabeyin Restaurant
Muharrem Çağlı

Established in 1958 in the city of Gaziantep, Mabeyin Restaurant is housed in an elegantly restored 19th century mansion in the Kısıklı district on the Asian side in Istanbul since 2003. Gourmet writer Anya von Bremzen described Mabeyin Restaurant as "one of the three best restaurants in Europe" in the US based Travel & Leisure magazine. "Definitely worth the trip" and "one of the best in the world" were the verdicts of Food & Wine magazine.

Mabeyin features the traditional, intricately spiced cuisine of Turkey's southeast. Particularly, dishes from the province of Gaziantep, are beautifully presented and worth tasting. In addition to traditional regional kebabs and grilled meats, don't miss the kebabs incorporating seasonal ingredients. Menu items also include some of the ethnic flavors of Ottoman and Turkish cuisine as well as vegetable dishes cooked in olive oil and a wide array of appetizers (meze).

Eski Kısıklı Caddesi No. 129 Kıksıklı, Istanbul
Tel: +90 216 422 55 80
info@mabeyin.com
www. mabeyin.com

Marianna Yerasimos

Born in Istanbul, where she still resides , Marianna Yerasimos is a Turk of Greek origin.

In her book, "500 Years of Ottoman Cuisine," Yerasimos writes, "As I wrote this book I learned a great deal, discovered little known aspects of the culture of which I'm a part of and found my realm of existence had been enriched." In her book, Yerasimos objective was to present an accurate overview of Ottoman cuisine from the 14th to the 20th century. She covered the main aspects of Ottoman Palace Cuisine, examined the influences of other cultures, explored the reasons and ways in which Ottoman cooking evolved over time. The book includes 99 recipes adapted for modern kitchens.

mayerasimos@superonline.com

Maximilian J.W. Thomae
Executive Chef - Pera Palas Hotel

Born in Germany in 1967 Maximilian J.W. Thomae was trained at Professional & Business School Miesbach in Germany. He began his career as a professional chef at Zum Alten Faehrhaus Restaurant, and went on to work in the kitchens of 1 Michelinstar Boettner Restaurant, 2 Michelin star Tantris Restaurant (Germany), InterContinental Resort Hotel Loipersdorf (Austria) and Crowne Plaza Holiday Inn (Istanbul), where he served as Executive Chef. From May 2006, to September 2009, Thomae was the Executive Chef at the Mövenpick IstanbulHotel, where he created many signature dishes. Since December 2009, he is the Executive Chef at the Pera Palas Hotel which is due to re-open in April 2010 once renovations are completed.

In 1996, Thomae was nominated to represent Turkey in the "Rotisserie of the Year" international competition held in New York City. During his stint as captain of the Turkish National Culinary Team, from 1996 to 1998, the team won numerous awards, including Salon Culinaire London and Malta. In 2007, Thomae was presented with a "Grand Achievement" award from TUSID (The Turkish Food Service, Laundry Equipment Manufacturers & Businessmen Association) and Hürriyet Newspaper named him the "Best Foreign Chef" in Turkey.

Through his interpretation of local ingredients and innovative culinary presentations, Maximilian J.W. Thomae has helped spearhead the Modern Turkish Cuisine movement.

Pera Palas Hotel
Meşrutiyet Caddesi No. 52
Tepebaşı-Beyoğlu, Istanbul
Tel: +90 212 222 80 90
www.perapalas.com

Mehmet Gök
Four Seasons Hotel Sultanahmet

Mehmet Gök has had a lifelong appreciation for simple, seasonal food and the effort that goes into preparing it. So so it's only natural that he insists upon using only the freshest local produce in the kitchens of Four Seasons Hotel Sultanahmet. "It's limiting at times," Mehmet Gök states, "but it means you end up with the best ingredients and food. It's different here from being a chef in London, where you can get a year-round supply of anything you want." Before he became Executive Chef at the Four Seasons Hotel Sultanahmet, Gök worked at the Fours Seasons property in Canary Wharf and was banquet manager for the seven restaurants at the Four Seasons Hotel Nile Plaza. Mehmet Gök knows he has a reputation to uphold, which is why he insists on assembling the best team possible as he represents both his hotel and his country.

www.fourseasons.com

Mehmet Gürs

Born in Tammisaari, Finland in 1969, Mehmet Gürs completed a B.S. in Hotel, Restaurant and Institutional Management at Johnson and Wales University in Providence, Rhode Island in 1993. Having worked as a chef at various well-known restaurants in Turkey and abroad until 2006, receiving numerous awards, Gürs opened Mikla Restaurant in the Beyoğlu district of Istanbul in October 2005. Ever since returning to Istanbul from the USA in1996, Gürs has been a trailblazer in contemporary cuisine and dining ambience. Mikla, the restaurant of which he is founder and chef, was soon named Istanbul's best restaurant for its inventive dishes, incomparable views, unstinting service and atmospheric music. Gürs sums up his cooking style as "contemporary Istanbul cuisine with Scandinavian influences". Fluent in Swedish, English and French, Mehmet Gürs is married and has a son.

mehmetgurs@istanbulyi.com

Mike Norman

Nevin Halıcı

Dr. Özge Samancı

Born in Cape Town and a graduate of the Johannesburg Hotel School of South Africa, Mike Norman has been passionate about food since childhood. Having worked as a chef for world-renowned Sun City, in his native country, the Relais & Chateaux group of hotels and restaurants, and Cunard Cruise Lines, Mike Norman has been living in Turkey for the past ten years.

Currently a partner of 360 Istanbul, one of the hottest restaurants in the city, Norman was formerly executive chef at the Çırağan Palace Kempinski, where he prepared dishes for such luminaries as Bill Clinton, Jacques Chirac, Nelson Mandela, Prince Charles and Liza Minnelli. Mike Norman also provides consultancy services for restaurant owners seeking to stand out from the crowd.

mike@360istanbul.com
www.360istanbul.com

Born in Konya, where she completed her early education, Nevin Halıcı studied Home Economics & Nutrition at Gazi University in Ankara, from 1970 to 1975. She completed her master's degree at Selçuk University in 1991 and her received her PhD at Gazi University in 1997. The author of numerous articles and papers published in Turkey and abroad, Halıcı has prepared exhibits on Turkish Cuisine, participated as a chef at various cooking demonstrations and prepared menus for congresses, seminars and other related r events. Her published works include: "Traditional Dishes of Konya" (1979); "Dishes of the Aegean Region" (1981); "Dishes of the Mediterranean Region" (1983); "Turkish Cuisine" (1985); "Nevin Halıcı's Turkish Cookbook" (1989); "Dishes of Southeast Anatolia" (1991); Classic Turkish Cuisine, From Sini to Tray" (1999); "A Study of Winter Foods in Konya" (2000); "Dishes of the Black Sea Region" (2001); Sufi Cuisine (2005); The Dishes and Food Culture of Konya" (2005); and "Mevlevi Cuisine" (2007).

nh@nevinhalici.com

Dr. Özge Samancı received her bachelor's and master's degrees from Robert College in Istanbul. In 2009, she received her PhD degree in history at the School for Advanced Studies in the Social Sciences in Paris, France. Prepared under the supervision of Gilles Veinstein, the topic of her thesis was "Food, Culinary Techniques and Tables Manners in 19th Century Istanbul". Since 2003, Dr. Samancı has been teaching at Yeditepe University, Gastronomy and Culinary Arts Deparment and she have been giving classes in Turkish and Ottoman Cuisine at the Istanbul Food Workshop since 2006.

Through her research, Özge Samancı seeks to examine the interaction of culture and cuisine, in particular, the influence modernization had on Ottoman culinary culture in the 19th century. She is the author of various works on Ottoman and Turkish food history and has participated in numerous colloquiums and seminars in France, Moroco, Uzbekistan and Turkey.

Dr. Özge Samancı is a member of th edtiorial board of the Turkish magazine Yemek ve Kültür (Food and Culture) and of the Friends of Jean-Louis Flandrin Society (Société des Amis de Jean-Louis Flandrin)

ozge@samanci.info
ozge@istanbulfoodworkshop.com
GSM: + 90 533 236 64 82

Pierre Jean Levy

A professional chef since 1975, Pierre Jean Levy began his career in Ozoir-la-Ferriere, on the outskirts of Paris. After working in France for 11 years, where he apprenticed for three years, Levy traveled to Switzerland, Sweden, China and Turkey. Levy has applied his expertise in French cuisine to Turkish food culture in order to create innovative dishes using all-natural, local ingredients.

A resident of Turkey since 2004, Pierre Jean Levy held positions at the fine dining Ulus 29 Restaurant as well as its sister establishments. Pierre Jean Levy loves to travel and is constantly on the lookout for new ideas and flavors.

shunfanpo@hotmail.com

Sevim Gökyıldız

As a result of her father's military career, Sevim Gökyıldız spent her childhood in various cities across Anatolia where she became acquainted with a wide variety of local Turkish dishes. Educated in part overseas, Gökyıldız also acquired firsthand experience of cooking French cuisine in Belgium and France.

20 years ago, after she retired from a 40-year career as Foreign Trade Director for a number of international companies, Gökyıldız began devoting herself to food writing. She has prepared food sections for many women's magazines, including Elele, Votre Beauté, Hello, Rapsodi, Kapris and Marie-Claire. Between 1996 and 1999, her own recipes were published in Lezzet and Ziyafet magazines. Through her on-the-job training at Cuisine et Vin de France with renowned chefs Eric Sola and Jacqueline Saulnier, Gökyıldız gained extensive experience and insight into food plating and photography.

Sevim Gökyıldız has dedicated herself to promoting Turkish cuisine abroad and has a French language website to that end. It is her belief that through such endeavours the overall Turkish economy and Turkish tourism in particular will benefit enormously.

Tel: + 90 212 280 95 51
GSM: + 90 532 457 81 82
sevimg@tr.net
sevim.gokyildiz@gmail.com
www.cuisine-turque.com

Sunset Grill & Bar
Hüseyin Aslan

The stunning views have been part of the best dining experience in Istanbul for the past 15 years at Sunset Grill & Bar. While the commitment to service has remained unchanged, the menu continues to evolve as it incorporates exciting new flavors.

In addition to its international and Turkish cuisine, Sunset Grill & Bar was the first venue in Turkey outside of Japanese restaurants to add a Sushi Bar. Japanese master chef Hiroki Takemura has since joined the long-term chefs at Sunset, where he presents offerings from New Japanese Cuisine.

Sunset Grill & Bar's exclusive wine cellars house a wide selection of rare wines that includes Petrus La Tache, Chateau Latour Sassiccaia and Opus One Chateau d'Yquem.

The finest champagnes in the world are also on offer, from Roederer Cristal to Krug. If you like, finish off a magnificent meal by selecting a Havana cigar from the Humidor, accompanied by Remy Martin Louis XIII rare cask cognac, a 40-year Springbank Malt or 1960s vintage port.

Adnan Saygun Caddesi Yol Sokak No. 2

Ulus Park - Ulus, Istanbul
Tel: + 90 212 287 03 57
info@sunsetgrillbar.com

Şans Restaurant
Ali Ekber Sarıgül

Surrounded by lush gardens and located in a lovely 2-story villa in the Levent district, Şans Restaurant is a dynamic place to experience the nightlife and gourmet culture of Istanbul. The Mediterranean and Turkish fare are complemented by a selection of choice wines and cigars. The bar on the 2nd floor is popular both as a post-work "happy hour" venue and as a lounge to relax with a cocktail before or after meals.

Chef Ali Ekber Sarıgül, otherwise known as 'Ali the Master', is behind the ever-evolving menu, which is updated every two months while still retaining such Şans classics as Stuffed Swiss Chard, Spinach Root, and Fish Chowder. The exclusive wine list complements the diverse menu and features the finest domestic vintages, as well as international selections from France, Italy, Chile, Australia and California. Şans Restaurant's commitment to top-quality service and food, as well as the further development of gastronomy in Turkey, was recognized by Chaine des Rotisseurs when Şans become one of a exclusive number of Turkish restaurants to become a member of the prestigious gastronomic society. (www.chaine-turkey.org).

Hacı Adil Caddesi, Palmiye Sokak No. 1
Birinci Levent 34330 Istanbul
Tel: + 90 212 280 38 38
sans@sansrestaurant.com

Takuhi Tovmasyan Zaman

Takuhi Tovmasyan Zaman was born in 1952 in the Yedikule district of Istanbul to a family originally from the Anatolian province of Çorlu. She was educated by Catholic nuns at Samatya Anarad Hığutyun Primary School and completed middle school at the Bakırköy Dadyan School. She then attended Sahakyan-Nunyan High School in Samatya. A mother of two, Zaman describes herself as a "mom" who was busy with the demands of home life and the ongoing education of her children at the conservatory.

15 years ago, when she decided the time had come to change this routine, her status as a 43 year-old housewife presented challenges in finding employment. Undaunted, Zaman began working as a typesetter at Aras Yayınevi, a publishing house founded by her family. Takuhi Tovmasyan Zaman went on to write a memoir/cookbook entitled "Memories of my Grandmother's Kitchen" (Aras Publications, October 2004, Istanbul). She also translated into Turkish a cookbook written by Boğos Piranyan nearly a century ago. Originally entitled "Nor Khoharar", it was released as "The Cook's Book" (Aras Publications, July 2008, Istanbul).

İstiklal Caddesi, Hıdivyal Palas, No. 231/Z
Tünel- Beyoğlu, Istanbul
takuhizaman@hotmail.com
takuhiz@gmail.com
info@arasyayincilik.com
www.arasyayincilik.com

Ümit Yüksel
Sheraton Istanbul Maslak Hotel

Born in Fatsa in 1975, Ümit Yüksel was trained at the Tekirdağ Anatolia Hotel and Tourism Vocational High School and completed his studies at the Vocational School of Hotel and Tourism. In 1997 he won a nationwide culinary competition and was named to the Turkish National Culinary Team. In various competitions held in Turkey and abroad, he won nine gold medals, 23 silver medals, 28 bronze medals, seven divisional firsts and various certificates.

Yüksel has participated in various events to promote Turkish cuisine in competitions held in Germany, England, Malta and Russia. He has also received special training in the cuisines of Italy, Lebanon, Germany and Greece. A member of the Platform of Young Turkish Chefs, Ümit Yüksel is contantly conducting and participating in research to further develop and diversify Turkish cuisine. He also supports various projects to encourage and help children at orphanages and reformatories who hope to become cooks one day. Ümit Yüksel continues to hold the position of Executive Chef at the Sheraton Istanbul Maslak Hotel.

Büyükdere Caddesi, No:. 233
Maslak 34398 Istanbul
Tel: +90 212 335 99 99
uyuksel@sheratonistanbulmaslak.com
www.sheraton.com/Istanbul

Vivet Rozales

Zeynep Çelikkan Kakınç

Vivet Rozales is the director of Süprem Catering, which was founded by her mother, Jinet Namer.

In addition to preparing menus suitable for invitational events, she acts as a menu consultant for hotels and restaurants. Rozales, who was at one time involved in the production of frozen foods, says they have a hard time keeping up with the demand for their "mosaic cake" and "borekitas". Vivet Rozales keeps up with the latest trends and says, "Presentation is of the utmost importance to us; our main emphasis is on quality, flavoır and elegance.

Yoncalı Sokak No. 10/a
Kuştepe- Mecidiyeköy , Istanbul
Tel: + 90 212 211 96 67
vivette@rozales.com

Zeynep Kakınç's family traces their roots to the Caucusus region, and she is of Circassian, Sapsih, Ubih and Abkhasian descent. Kakınç once ran her own public relations firm. An executive board member of the Friends of the Kitchen Association, Zeynep Çelikkan Kakınç contributed articles on food and drink to La Cucina Italiana magazine and is conducting research into Circassian and Abkhasian cuisine.

GSM: + 90 532 212 35 52
zeynepkakinc@gmail.com

*L*ocated in Tepebaşı - or otherwise known as Pera, the Istanbul Culinary Institute (ICI) is in the heart of Istanbul's busy commercial district. ICI was conceived with a mission to teach, develop and promote Turkish cuisine nationally and internationally. It is a cooking school, training restaurant and gourmet food store, all under one roof. Open since 2007, it is already a favorite spot for Istanbul's food enthusiasts, as well as "an addictive neighborhood eatery" as many regulars cotend. Additionally, increasing international media coverage continues to direct the spotlight on ICI's many activities and programs.

The Istanbul Culinary Institute is equally committed to professional and amateur culinary programs tailored to answer different needs and objectives. The Chefs School, a highly competitive professional certificate program, focuses on Turkish and Mediterranean cuisines with hands-on training at ICI's restaurant. The purpose is to equip its students with real-life experiences in every stage and station involved in the complex workings of a commercial kitchen. Thus, graduates gain experience and confidence and as professionals are prepared for careers in the culinary industry. On the other hand, programs for amateurs include a variety of workshops and short courses held in four different kitchens of the Institute. Here, in small groups, participants are taught specific kitchen skills and have the opportunity to experiment with guest chefs. But, above all, they are cooking, sharing experiences, eating, drinking and just having fun. These programs are further supplemented with a variety of seminars, thematic culinary tours and gastronomic events with celebrated chefs from around the world.

Foremost among the founding principles of ICI is the belief in ecological responsibility and sustainable agriculture as the most important premises of a viable culinary culture. ICI seeks to raise public awareness of these issues and upholds a strong commitment to using only the freshest, seasonal ingredients from reliable sources. In line with this commitment, a significant portion of the produce, fruits and herbs used in its kitchens are grown naturally and free of chemicals and hormones, at the ICI-affiliated Saros gardens and orchards in the Northern Aegean of Turkey.

ICI's fundamental philosophy is that there is not only a professional, but also an ethical dimension to cooking and shares these beliefs with its students, staff and customers on a daily basis.

Index